# Extraordinary praise for Patti S. Webster's
## IT HAPPENED IN CHURCH

"I love this book. Not only is it inspirational and uplifting, but Patti has a way of laughing her way through life's ups and downs. . . . Completely infectious!"

—Halle Berry, Academy Award–winning actress

"God has blessed Patti with the ability to be a great communicator and to be a bridge between people from all walks of life. I'm so happy that this book has come to life, because through it, she's able to share with us stories that we can all identify with. Stories that will make us laugh, smile and remember. Patti, you better work, girl!"

—Patti LaBelle, Grammy Award–winning musician
and best-selling author

"It's a real blessing to be connected to someone whose work screams excellence, is a person of integrity, and most importantly, whose light continues to shine brightly for God in an industry where darkness is most prevalent. We're glad we know you, Patti."

—Mary Mary, Grammy Award–winning gospel duo

"In times of stress in an ever-changing world where pressure is evident and pain is real WE NEED TO LAUGH! As the Bible says, 'A merry heart doeth good like a medicine.' Patti

caught the vision and didn't hesitate to embrace it and now we all can be healed, and dat's what's up!!"

—Tye Tribbett, musician and founder of the
Grammy-nominated and
Stellar Award–winning gospel group
Tye Tribbett & G.A.

*"It Happened in Church* is an amusing collection of anecdotes and stories revolving around the church. Patti Webster has put her loving spirit into this book, which is sure to bring a smile—and a chuckle—to each reader. It should be enjoyed by the entire family."

—Janet Jackson, Grammy Award–winning musician

"Patti Webster is an amazing friend, brilliant colleague and excellent author. Her book wittily offers a unique and clever viewpoint about church humor."

—Usher Raymond, Grammy Award–winning musician

It Happened
in Church

# It Happened in Church

## Stories of Humor from the Pulpit to the Pews

Patti S. Webster

*with a Foreword by Pastor Donnie McClurkin*

SOULS OF MY SISTERS BOOKS
Kensington Publishing Corp.
http://www.kensingtonbooks.com

SOULS OF MY SISTERS books are published by

Kensington Publishing Corp. and Souls of My Sisters, Inc.
850 Third Avenue
New York, NY 10022

ISBN-13: 978-0-7582-2706-5
ISBN-10: 0-7582-2706-X

First Trade Paperback Printing: September 2008
10  9  8  7  6  5  4  3  2  1

Printed in the United States of America

My Lord and Savior Jesus Christ—the One I love more than the breath He has given me. It would take an innumerable amount of pages to share the appreciation I have for God and His unbelievable love for me. He's given me hope beyond life, joy beyond the tears and love on this side of heaven. This book is dedicated to Him for the idea, the vision, the direction and the laughter. As Mother Teresa once said, "I am a little pencil in the hand of a writing God."

Adeline Harley and Vatus Webster, my wonderful grandmothers. Although you are gone, in my heart, you will NEVER be forgotten. I wish my friends had gotten to know you, as you were two of the most instrumental influences in my life. You were also two of the funniest women I have ever met—even though I don't think you realized it. Your faith in God, your undying devotion and love for your family and your deep reverence and love for all things holy continue to be an important foundation to the woman I am today. I will love you always.

Mom (Pastor Pat) and Dad (Pastor Jack, aka Poppa), no words could ever express the love I have for you and how you demonstrate that love no matter what. Thank you for your Godly example. Thank you for your prayers. Thank you for your encouragement. Thank you for never giving up on me. Thank you for showing me how to laugh. Thank you for teaching me the ways of the Lord. Thank you for EVERYTHING. I LOVE YOU!!!!

And to my brothers and sisters—Shelly, Scott, Laurie, Al, Lori and Peter—thank you for always being there to support me, encourage me and love me. Thanks for the many days of laughter (and of course, Peter's infectious laugh didn't hurt!). I love you madly! May God bless each of you exceedingly abundantly above all that you can ask or think.

# Contents

# FOREWORD

## Pastor Donnie McClurkin

This is an entrance into the world of humor and pointed reflections of the church combining the human side with the Holy. You will laugh and, in many cases, find some of the scenarios hard to believe . . . but all of it will have you see the present (experiences) and past (scripture events) come together in reflections.

*It Happened in Church* is a wonderful read, but also reflective and insightful. So often, the church is looked upon as an imposing institution, yet the goal of all churches is to create a community of love and understanding. A community full of faithful and caring people. What better way to connect with the community than with humor? Humor also allows us to get through some of the most difficult moments in our lives. And when combined with faith, humor can become a life-sustaining element. Studies have even shown that those who believe—as well as those who take time out for good, hearty laughter—live longer. Both humor and faith help to relieve stress, rejuvenate us and help us realize that troubles do pass.

*It Happened in Church* includes insight about humor from

famous quotes, to true-life stories, to biblical accounts and re-flections from some of today's leading religious figures. Whether we always recognize them or not, daily life is full of humor-ous moments—even when we are in church. God never meant for His children just to be sullen and serious. God wants us to enjoy all aspects of our lives. To learn—and sometimes laugh—at our mistakes and situations.

And yes, we're sure Jesus, too, enjoyed a good laugh.

# ACKNOWLEDGMENTS

There are so many people I have to thank and I unfortunately can't name everyone. . . . I wish I could. But if I forget anyone, please, please charge it to my head and not to my heart. For everyone who shared a story, a thought, an idea, a note, a word of encouragement, a prayer or two or three or four—THANK YOU!

To Candace Sandy and Dawn Marie Daniels: You are two wonderful women of God and I cannot thank you enough for believing in me and helping me to make a dream come true. I am so glad God crossed our paths. I love you both and expect us to do great things together by keeping laughter in the body of Christ! Thank you to Walter and Steve Zacharius, Laurie Parkin and Rakia Clark, and the Kensington Publishing Corp. staff.

To Randy Vaughan: My savior, my brother, my friend, my encourager and my supporter—you have shown me what true friendship is all about. I am speechless for all that you have done to make sure this book was written. You have a friend for life. More Smith Wigglesworth books on the way!

To Maria Vaughan: For being so gracious in allowing your husband to be there for me. Thank You & Love You!

To Denise Kearse: You have gone beyond the call of duty. I don't take all that you do, to make my crazy life sane, for granted. You have such a giving heart and I know that the Lord sees you for who you really are—a wonderful woman of God who will give of her last to make someone like me shine brighter. I love you, but above all, I thank you.

To Inez and Silvester Avant: You are two of the most special people in my life. I thank you for loving me as much as you do. Go Giants! (LOL)

To Gerrod White: Thank you for making those days easier when I needed to be in "writing mode" and those subtle reminders that "you have writing to do." Thank you also for the many stories you gathered for me. I appreciate you always, but still hate the Bulls!

To my W&W Crew: Aliya Crawford, Kitara Garner, Jacinda Chen, Toray Butler, Linda Stokes, Phil Jun—I could never ask for a better group of friends who lift me up, hold me up and force me to do things I don't want to do! (LOL) Love you so much! Thanks for everything!

To my nieces and nephews: Ted, Mary, Michael, Vanessa, Ashley, Kelvin—each of you have such special gifts. I pray that you see yourselves as God sees you—wonderfully made, marvelous in His eyes and created for His glory! And to my great-niece, Sydnee—may I always be an example of God's love and may all of us teach you that "the fear of the Lord is the beginning of wisdom." Love you!

To my sisterhood, motherhood and cousinhood (in alphabetical order by first name—LOL): Alicia Carmen, Amanda Back, Angel DeGrasse, Anita Ford, Audra Washington, Ayeshia

Burdette, Carol Williams, Charlotte Castillo, Chrysa Chin, Dana Frank, Dee Walker, Denise McIver, Halle Berry, Karen Lee, Jen Watson, Jennifer Young, Joann White, Kim Scott, Lana Walker, Leah Wilcox, Leslie Short, Lorissa Clark, Marion Gomez, Melanie Carter, Michelle Curry, Neicy Tribbett, Neily Dickerson, Nekeda Newell Hall, Patti Logan, Penny McDonald, Roberta Schenck, Roberta Young, Rose Goring, Sharhonda Stockman, Sharon Heyward, Sharon Young, Sheila Coates, Sheila Jamison, Sheila Jones, Sheri Riley, Suzette Sanders, Teresa Caldwell, Theresa Frank, Tracie Mayer, Valerie "Daisy" Haynie, Vernessa Gates, Vinlyn Beckles, Vivian Chew, Yvette Noel Schure—you truly are God's angels. Thank you for your gifts of sisterhood, friendship, your gifts of love and your gifts of laughter! Who knew God could give one woman more than forty angels!!!!!

To my SPC family: You guys rock! Sorry, you guys worship! Thank you for your prayers, your prayers, your prayers and your prayers! Lord knows I needed and still need them. I couldn't ask for a better church family—and I am anticipating the great things God has in store for each of you. Keep Him first always, love each other beyond Sunday and remember to never compromise who you are in Him.

A special shout out to the SPC "A Chosen Generation" Youth Ministry: God couldn't have blessed me more if I had birthed each of you myself. Thank you for loving me, encouraging me, trusting me and sharing with me. I love you guys soooo much and all I desire is that you live your life to the fullest—with God leading the way!

To my dear friend Pastor Donnie McClurkin: You graciously give of yourself always. I hope that you realize beyond being an anointed man of God, an incredible singer and soul-stirring preacher, you are a comedian at heart. You have given me such laughter over the years, and you are so instrumental to the body of Christ. I know that God has so much more in store for you and I am looking forward to seeing the continued blessings of the Lord upon your life. I love you and thank God for you.

To Roger Holmes: You are a man of honor and a true man of your word. Thank you for just opening up your Rolodex to help my first endeavor and always opening up your heart whenever I call. May God bless you always!

A special thanks to Patti LaBelle, Tichina Arnold, Richard Smallwood, Vanessa Bell Armstrong, Ayiesha Woods, Dr. Creflo A. Dollar and Mary Mary for adding your star power to my first book. You didn't have to do it, but I'm so glad you did! Thanks for the stories—can't wait to call you all again for Part II!

And to everyone who will read this book, gift this book or share it with a friend—thank you for investing your money, but most importantly, your time. I hope you will laugh and laugh and laugh and laugh and continue to laugh again.

# CHAPTER ONE

## It Happened in Church

He will fill your mouth with laughter and your lips
with shouts of joy.

—Job 8:21

*Humor is also a way of saying something serious.*

—T.S. Eliot

## A KEEN SENSE OF HUMOR

According to Billy Graham, "a keen sense of humor helps us to overcome the unbecoming, understand the unconventional, tolerate the unpleasant, overcome the unexpected and outlast the unbearable."

*The Bible says: She is clothed with strength and dignity; she can laugh at the days to come.* (Proverbs 31:25, NIV)

### Reflection

Emotion replaces emotion. Although we can be confused at times, we are not often displaying two or more emotions at the same time. We're not angry and happy, or crying and laughing. Typically these emotions take place one at a time. Although the switching of these emotions can take place at light speed, most importantly when we can laugh when we could be angry, sad, despondent or depressed reinforces the importance of humor, more so than in just getting a quick laugh. Our joy can bring us through adversity and is expressed in our ability to laugh.

The unlikeliest venue for laughter would probably be, in some minds, the church. Some would even suggest the Bible's admonition against jesting as evidence against having fun and laughter. While not a serious or hotly debated subject today, during the thirteenth century in France at the University of Paris, a conference was actually held to determine if Jesus had ever laughed.

Interestingly the Bible is seemingly backed up by science that suggests laughter is actually good for the physical health.

The Bible says: *A cheerful heart is good medicine, but a crushed spirit dries up the bones.* (Proverbs 17:22, NIV)

It's no mystery in the world of medicine that laughter has been proven to be actually good for your physical health.

Throughout this book we will witness real-life hilarious moments of events that have taken place within those sacred walls of worship. Whether it was a wedding, funeral, baby dedication or regular Sunday morning service. Those unexpected and funny situations do arise, causing laughter and joy even during the most stressful moments.

Oftentimes it's asked, "Is there humor in the Bible?" The answer is yes, of course. British mathematician and philosopher Alfred North Whitehead once said, "The total absence of humor from the Bible is one of the most singular things in all of literature." He could not have been more wrong. Subsequently, if there is humor in the Bible, then there can be humor in the church.

We can find humor in almost every walk of life, depending

on the person. Does God laugh? If so, what does He laugh at? We can't imagine He doesn't. At the same time, laughter is an emotional release. On a physiological level, it is probably necessary at various stages in life, as are other emotional characteristics. After all, He created the emotional reaction, and in addition, through biblical inspiration in Ecclesiastes 3:4, there is "a time to weep and a time to laugh."

Interesting as it may sound, slipping on a banana peel may not be that funny at the time of the incident. Concerns for the fallen individual would definitely cause us to put the comedic part of this scenario on the back burner. Some of our most humorous moments occur without the intent to solicit a laugh. The young child who repeats something the parent said in private about someone else. While these little slipups of our children are most embarrassing at the time and uncomfortable, they are hilarious to recount while sitting around the table at Thanksgiving dinner.

This same principle can be applied to many passages found within the Bible. Many of the episodes found in the scriptures have the same tendency to cause laughter when looked at from another perspective and possibly at a later date. There weren't too many stand-up comedians in ancient Mesopotamia. The Screen Writer's Guild also did not exist. Subsequently, there are no explicit attempts at humor in the Bible. Are there occasions that something is funny? Absolutely.

Finding the humor in a situation or person does not undermine the seriousness of an event. Most of us can probably remember a horrific incident and still find something humorous surrounding the event. In fact, it's at those times that laughter may be the most welcome. Most modern biblical scholars will attest to the presence of humor in the Bible. Whether they are explicit or implicit, intentional or by accident, funny things have their residence in what many consider the Holy Scriptures. Of course, for many, finding these scriptural funny treasures is next to impossible. Why is it so difficult to pick up and read this ancient book of history, proverbs and answers and not find something to laugh at?

First, some would venture to say that it isn't an absence of humorous events in the Bible, but the presence of our own tradition and religiosity. Understandably, it is difficult for people to imagine those things we hold high and dear to be anything less than holy and perfect. We cannot imagine that there was a day when our grandparents had a crush, or our pastor may have thought a Hollywood celebrity was dreamy. We must remove ourselves from the multigenerational prejudice of seeing the Bible as only a serious, judgmental and sacred document. It is a composite of sixty-six documents composed by humans who have cried, lied, smirked, hiccupped, belched, sung badly, become angry, got scared at night and laughed when they saw a monkey drop a banana on the other monkey's head at the bottom of the tree.

Second, the blockage of our vision of the Bible's humor is one of a linguistic nature. The Bible's three principal languages are Aramaic, Hebrew and Greek. These texts, as far as the English language is concerned, are now translated in at least one hundred different versions. Not only is the language itself an aid in obscuring the humor in the texts, but its antiquity as well. The youngest parts of our Bible writings occur approxi-

mately nineteen hundred years ago, while the oldest are approximately four thousand years old. Adding to this dilemma
is the fact that many are transcribing events that took place long
before they were actually penned. Such is the case with Job,
the Bible's oldest book. While probably not written by Job, its
editing and compilation may have taken place hundreds of years
afterward.

There is a story of a woman and her son who were experiencing a bad day—the burial of her husband and her son's father. While the processional passed by the casket containing the
body, the wife became increasingly distraught and had to be
assisted to the car leading to the repast. After being taken to the
limousine, she began to laugh. Her son, thinking that his mom
had possibly gone mad, asked her if she was okay. She laughed
again and said she almost lost her dentures while crying and
thinking her deceased husband would've probably gotten a
good laugh out of it. This is an example of the type of harsh
and painful realities in life that later may cause us to smile and
even laugh.

Throughout the book are arguably some of the funniest moments in the Bible. Understandably many may not find any of
the stories or settings humorous. Their tendency may be to look
at all of the passages with a serious eye. They probably wouldn't
be reading this book in that event. Obviously the stories out-
lined were not intended to be funny initially.

Many of the biblical stories are accompanied by additional
details to allow many readers who are not fully aware of the
various circumstances surrounding our—sometimes—comical characters to better understand them. Most will be preceded

by a brief scenario of where they are in a specific situation. Afterward a follow-up will conclude what may have happened after the laughter died.

Life is so good and beautiful. Even when we look back at the harshness that may have engulfed us at some point, the overcoming brings about joy in our heart. So open up the following pages and begin to live, love and laugh. In the words of Jesus, *"Rejoice and be exceeding glad"* (Matthew 5:12).

# CHAPTER TWO

## Faith the Size of a Mustard Seed

❧

*When you get into a tight place and everything goes against you, till it seems as though you could not hold on a minute longer, never give up then, for that is just the place and time that the tide will turn.*

—Harriett Beecher Stowe

The mustard seed is considered one of the smallest seeds on earth. When Jesus talks about faith using this illustration, He is trying to teach us that it doesn't take much to tug on the hem of His garment, such as the woman with the issue of blood tugged. We are often led to believe that the kind of faith God is requiring of us is the mother lode of all faiths. This leads many of us not even to try the measure of faith given to us. Most Christians would be totally surprised that the faith they already possess is enough to move a mountain. That this same exact measure of faith is actually considered a gift of the Spirit.

First Corinthians 13:2 says:

*If I have the gift of prophecy and can fathom all mysteries and all knowledge, and if I have a faith that can move mountains, but have not love, I am nothing.* (NIV)

Then again, Matthew 17:19–21 says:

*Then the disciples came to Jesus in private and asked, "Why couldn't we drive it out?" He replied, "Because you have so little faith. I tell you the truth, if you have faith as small as a mustard seed, you can say to this mountain, 'Move from here to there' and it will move. Nothing will be impossible for you."* (NIV)

It's apparent that the words of Matthew and Jesus agree. Yet many Christians dismiss themselves from Matthew's description of the gift of faith, believing it to be only for the pillars of faith. I used to think that way. I never felt I had the faith to accomplish anything through God. But as I've grown more in love with Christ, my faith has increased and I can see the miraculous hand of God moving in my life in ways I would never expect. It doesn't take much—just a small amount of your belief with a large dose of God's power. So move that mountain, my friend. For with God, all things are possible.

*The angels are so enamored of the language that is spo-
ken in heaven, that they will not distort their lips with
the hissing and unmusical dialects of men, but speak their
own, whether there be any who understand it or not.*

—Ralph Waldo Emerson

## SWEEPING THROUGH THE CITY

In the neighborhood of the church where I grew up, located
in Somerville, New Jersey, there lived a woman whose mind,
many would agree, was not necessarily stable. During one of
our Sabbath services many years ago on a typical afternoon,
Ms. Alice came into Shiloh Pentecostal Church with a mop and
bucket and said she just came to clean up all the sh** in the
street. After she said her piece and announced her plans, she
left. Interestingly, God gives grace at those kinds of moments
as no one got upset. I guess we wanted to see if she'd really
clean it up.

**Apostle Joel Rudolph** is the senior pastor of Christian Fellowship Center in Paterson, New Jersey.

The Bible says: *"Woe to me!" I cried. "I am ruined! For I
am a man of unclean lips, and I live among a people of
unclean lips, and my eyes have seen the King, the LORD*

Almighty." Then one of the seraphs flew to me with a live
coal in his hand, which he had taken with tongs from the
altar. With it he touched my mouth and said, "See, this
has touched your lips; your guilt is taken away and your
sin atoned for." (Isaiah 6:5–7)

## Reflection

*Then we'll go sweepin' through the city,*
*Where my captain has gone before*
*and we're gonna sit down by the banks of the river;*
*I won't be back,*
*I won't be back,*
*I won't be back no more, no more.*

The song above, made so famous by Shirley Caesar, still
speaks volumes today. While the song refers to saints going to
a city already swept, it had to be swept by someone. Like many
churchgoers, we wait for society to take care of its mess. Yet as
Christians, we are called to be the light of the world. This is
difficult if we stay hidden under a bushel or in our churches.
How great a testimony and a harvesting it would be if we were
the ones who cleaned and swept the streets of the world.

*Laughter is the closest distance between two people.*

—Victor Borge

## AMEN, PHARAOH!

How many times have you been in church where you have prayed that the preacher would just sit down? It's almost like you are listening to a verbal rendition of the New York Marathon when the preacher seems to go on and on and on and on and on. Well, on one Sunday morning, a visiting minister was being very long-winded. Even worse, every time he would make a good point during his sermon and a member of the congregation responded with "Amen" or "That's right, preacher," he would get wound up even more and launch into another lengthy discourse. This went on and on for two hours. Finally, the host pastor started responding to every few sentences with "Amen, Pharaoh!" The guest minister wasn't sure what that meant, but after several more "Amen, Pharaohs," he finally concluded his very lengthy sermon. After the service concluded and the congregation had left, the visiting minister turned to his host and asked, "What exactly did you mean when you said, 'Amen, Pharaoh!'?" His host replied, "I was telling you to let my people go!"

**Randy Vaughan** is an author and a member of Shiloh Pentecostal Church, Inc.–Christian Love Center in Somerville, New Jersey.

The Bible says: *And there sat in a window a certain young man named Eutychus, being fallen into a deep sleep: and as Paul was long preaching, he sunk down with sleep, and fell down from the third loft, and was taken up dead. And Paul went down, and fell on him, and embracing him said, Trouble not yourselves; for his life is in him.* (Acts 20:9–10)

## Reflection

The long-winded preacher did not just manifest himself in the twentieth century; the Bible tells us in Acts that Paul was preaching so long, a young man named Eutychus fell asleep and subsequently fell out the window. What could Paul have possibly been talking about so long? Did you know that Jesus's Sermon on the Mount times out at no more than ten minutes and is one of the most powerful sermons ever preached? Some of the most powerful punches have been delivered in the shortest span of time. So don't always look for a long dissertation when you come to church; look for God in the still, small voice and in a brief moment of time He'll be there.

*Life's most urgent question is: What are you doing for others?*

—Martin Luther King, Jr.

## DID HE SAY TITHES OR . . .

On a Sunday morning at Christian Fellowship Center a little old woman was visiting. She appeared to be a normal sweet-looking elderly woman. As the service proceeded, announcements were done and songs were sung. Eventually a minor lull in the service happened. During that time she stood up and asked, "Where's the pastor?" When Pastor Joel Rudolph stood up, she said that she had to put her tithing in the man of God's hands and proceeded to walk toward him. As she got closer toward him, she took her hand and started bouncing her breast—and said, "The Devil had stole one of my titties but he can't take the other one." She came up with the tithe, but he said that he didn't want to touch it. Most were not sure if he didn't want to touch the tithe or the . . . well, you get it. In any case he touched nothing. He managed to keep a straight face, but everyone else in the congregation was in hysterics.

**Apostle Joel Rudolph** is the senior pastor of Christian Fellowship Center in Paterson, New Jersey.

The Bible says: *Therefore, I urge you, brothers, in view of God's mercy, to offer your bodies as living sacrifices, holy and pleasing to God—this is your spiritual act of worship. Do not conform any longer to the pattern of this world, but be transformed by the renewing of your mind. Then you will be able to test and approve what God's will is—his good, pleasing and perfect will.* (Romans 12:1–2)

## Reflection

"All to Jesus, I surrender; All to Him I freely give; I will ever love and trust Him, In His presence daily live." These are the words to a very popular hymn sung in thousands of church congregations every Sunday morning. From the previous story it's apparent that the elderly, possibly senile, woman felt there was nothing she wouldn't give to the Lord. When we realize that we truly can't hoard what God has freely given us, then we, too, will find it easier to give Him all.

*Every man's work, whether it be literature or music or
pictures or architecture or anything else, is always a
portrait of himself.*

—Samuel Butler

## NOT EXACTLY THE WALLS OF JERICHO

In this small Spanish-speaking Pentecostal church in cen-
tral New Jersey, Pastor Ramon Rodriguez was preaching his
heart out. He knew he was on fire. The Spirit of God was in
him and he could not contain the fire that was burning in his
bones.

The faithful seemed to be more intent than ever. They were
hanging on to every word he was saying. He knew this because
they had stopped shouting out praises. What he didn't realize
was that the wall behind him was beginning to move. Immediately the worshippers let out a collective shout. He knew he
was reaching them now and he began to preach even harder.

For whatever reason he just stopped momentarily—he seemed
to get it now. He turned around to see that the wall had fallen
down and that the neighbors in the adjacent yard were now
paying attention to his message as well. He looked back at the
congregates and let out a huge laugh and began to preach where
he had left off.

Funny thing is he probably would not have remodeled the

dilapidated building if the wall had not come down. Apparently while he was just praying for the Lord to keep the worship facilities together, the congregation was praying that the wall would fall so they could get a new church.

**Randy Vaughan** is an author and a member of Shiloh Pentecostal Church, Inc.–Christian Love Center in Somerville, New Jersey.

The Bible says: *By faith the walls of Jericho fell, after the people had marched around them for seven days.* (Hebrews 11:30, NIV)

*And I tell you that you are Peter, and on this rock I will build my church, and the gates of Hades will not overcome it. And I will give you the keys of the kingdom of heaven; whatever you bind on earth will be bound in heaven, and whatever you loose on earth will be loosed in heaven.* (Matthew 16:18–19, NIV)

## Reflection

Some of God's greatest moves of His Spirit have been in the unlikeliest places. He seems to take joy in allowing people to find Him in normal places. The Azusa Street revival was held in a former stable. The Great Awakening revival took place outside. The Great Kentucky revival took place in the hills and mountains outdoors. The church itself began in an upper room of Solomon's temple and eventually poured outside. It's easier said than done, not to confine our God to architecture, but it's what we continue to do. While no one is knocking a great building, let's not forget that mankind changed with the birth of a child in a stable.

# Laugh Stop

Children at a Catholic elementary school wrote the following statements about the Bible. They have not been retouched or corrected (i.e., incorrect spelling has been left in).

1. In the first book of the bible, Guinessis, God got tired of creating the world, so he took the Sabbath off.
2. Adam and Eve were created from an apple tree. Noah's wife was called Joan of Ark. Noah built an ark, which the animals come on to in pears.
3. Lot's wife was a pillar of salt by day, but a ball of fire by night.
4. The Jews were a proud people and throughout history they had trouble with the unsympathetic Genitals.
5. Samson was a strong man who let himself be led astray by a Jezebel like Delilah.
6. Samson slayed the Philistines with the axe of the Apostles.
7. Moses led the Hebrews to the Red Sea, where they made unleavened bread which is bread without any ingredients.
8. The Egyptians were all drowned in the dessert. Afterwards, Moses went up on Mount Cyanide to get the ten amendments.

9. The first commandment was when Eve told Adam to eat the apple.

10. The seventh commandment is thou shalt not admit adultery.

11. Moses died before he ever reached Canada. Then Joshua led the Hebrews in the battle of Geritol.

*If you judge people, you have not time to love them.*

—Mother Teresa

## NO SMOKING IN CHURCH?

Paula White tells a story of a young woman she met at *The Tyra Banks Show* who came to her church. Actually the woman and a friend were guests of her Satisfied Woman Ladies Retreat one summer. Paula states, "They were sitting in the front row during one of our 'marathon' services. I was speaking about the love of God, how you are not a product of where you came from and how love activates faith, and my heart filled with joy as I looked down to see that the young woman was so into the message with tears streaming down her face! Now remember, she didn't grow up in church and has never heard of 'church protocol'—she did the cutest thing—she was so wrapped up and consumed with the ministry that she reached down and pulled out a cigarette and started smoking in the front row! Of course, some of my ushers approached her to escort her outside (Florida is a clean air state) but I stopped them. . . . 'Don't interrupt her—the Spirit of God is moving and dealing with her!' I still smile today thinking about her purity and innocence in that moment. I am so thankful to have played a part in her destiny!"

**Paula Michelle White** is a preacher, life coach, author, motivational speaker and former senior pastor of Without Walls International Church in Tampa, Florida. She has her own television ministry and has authored numerous best-selling books. In addition, she has become a spiritual advisor to many celebrities including Donald Trump, Michael Jackson and Tyra Banks.

The Bible says: *Not what goes into the mouth defiles a man; but what comes out of the mouth, this defiles a man.* (Matthew 15:11, NIV)

## Reflection

The worst time to make judgment of someone is when God is working with that person in a special way. Often when a person is being convicted and spoken to by God, through various means, it is also the time when that person may appear to be at his or her worst. It's at that time that the person may even "kick against the pricks," as Paul had done. Waiting to receive that person with loving arms is the way God wants us to receive the new convert into His kingdom.

*People who worship only themselves begin to look like monuments. Too bad they had to go so soon.*

—Vanna Bonta

## FALSE TEETH PROPHET

In a church of about thirty worshippers, there was a small service of two churches combined for a rare evening service. The visiting speaker had been speaking for about thirty minutes. Apparently he was beginning to get to that point, as in so many African-American churches, where the minister begins to really get down. We call it hoopin' and hollerin'—getting the crowd further into the message.

He was on a roll. He had them right where he wanted them. The hallelujahs were beginning to sound out, and just as he was about to put his foot in it . . . whoops, his teeth fell out. Quickly he slid them back into his mouth. At first he had a slight look of embarrassment. However, it was soon extinguished, as he felt confident that no one caught the slip. The only problem is everyone caught the mishap, including his wife. Everyone just played it off, pretending not to see him standing right in front of the pulpit—a hard job to pull off.

This minor inconvenience did not stop him, as he continued to pour out God's Word as if it were the last message before the Rapture. I'm sure whatever the offering he received that night was utilized about fifteen minutes later at an all-night drugstore for a quality tube of denture adhesive. Of course, all those in attendance laughed their heads off on the ride home.

**Chantel Howard** is the corporate travel director and church treasurer of Union Baptist Church, South River, New Jersey.

The Bible says: *When they see the purity and reverence of your lives. Your beauty should not come from outward adornment . . . Instead, it should be that of your inner self, the unfading beauty of a gentle and quiet spirit, which is of great worth in God's sight.* (1 Peter 3:2–4, NIV)

## Reflection

While there is humor in the previous story's sequence of events, we should seek to understand how the minister found himself in this situation. He was more concerned that those in fellowship were more focused on him rather than the inspiration he was delivering. Unfortunately he is partially right. There are those who come to church in a ritualistic fashion—just to be a spectator, laugh and socialize. And there are those who purely come to hear the voice of the Lord through the man and woman of God—so they truly see or hear nothing else by the movement of God through the building. I can't wait to get to a day when all those who believe in the Lord Jesus Christ won't care about who is looking at them, won't worry about who is sitting next to them or what my friend is wearing, but will be entrenched in the presence of God and desire only to do like the angels on a daily basis while they are around the throne of God, crying out, "Holy, Holy, Holy!"

*Let your mind alone, and see what happens.*

—Virgil Thomson

## CATCH ME IF YOU CAN

In some Pentecostal churches many people are known to "fall out under the Spirit" or "be slain in the Spirit." They attribute this phenomenon to the overwhelming power of God touching them. Many will attest to its necessity in trying to deal with a certain area in their lives.

As an elder in this congregation, during prayer time, one of my assignments was to "catch" these individuals as they were slain. I should explain that although I assisted in this part of the service, I was not an enthusiastic participant in what I felt was just an overload of emotional display. This is not to say that the miraculous didn't occur. Let's just say that, in my opinion, most of the time this "slaying" was simply emotional.

In our congregation we had this one woman who seemed to be always "going through." Few of us could determine what this "going through" consisted of at any given time. Anyway, she was always in the prayer line to get hands laid on her.

Fortunately on this particular Sunday not too many people came up for prayer. At least not the ones who always fell out. So I felt comfortable in sitting this one out as a catcher. Unfortunately, "going through" decided she couldn't pass up another touch and went into the line at the last second. It didn't take her long. However, because no one was standing behind her, she began to backpedal all the way to the back of the church. I had to get up and outrun her before she crashed into something. I thought about opening the door and letting her just careen out in the front of the church. I imagine that "going through" after that always made sure there was a catcher behind her before she felt the Spirit move.

Author unknown.

The Bible says: *Then He said, "Go out, and stand on the mountain before the LORD." And behold, the LORD passed by, and a great and strong wind tore into the mountains and broke the rocks in pieces before the LORD, but the LORD was not in the wind; and after the wind an earthquake, but the LORD was not in the earthquake; and after the earthquake a fire, but the LORD was not in the fire; and after the fire a still small voice.* (1 Kings 19:11–12, NIV)

## Reflection

There is an old saying, "We tend to find what we're looking for." What this means is that if there is something we want in our lives, but that particular thing isn't available, we place it there within our imagination. Just like in the above passage from the Bible. Elijah looked for God's voice in some phenomenal manner instead of realizing that God speaking to us in any manner is incredible. Sometimes God has something for us that may not be what we're looking for, but it may be what we need. Instead of His voice out of the sky, it may be the silence that we may mistake as being lonely. So no matter what you are "going through," God will speak to you and all you have to do is listen.

# Laugh Stop

### God's Getting Better

A little girl was sitting on her grandfather's lap as he read her a bedtime story. From time to time, she would take her eyes off the book and reach up to touch his wrinkled cheek. She was alternately stroking her own cheek, then his again. Finally she spoke up, "Grandpa, did God make you?" "Yes, sweetheart," he answered. "God made me a long time ago." "Oh." She paused. "Grandpa, did God make me, too?" "Yes, indeed, honey," he said. "God made you just a little while ago." Feeling their respective faces again, she observed, "God's getting better at it, isn't he?"

### Mommy's Prayer

A mother invited some people to dinner. At the table, she turned to her six-year-old daughter and said, "Would you like to say the blessing?" "I wouldn't know what to say," the girl replied. "Just say what you hear Mommy say," she answered. The daughter bowed her head and said, "Lord, why on earth did I invite all these people to dinner?"

## Cover Your Wife

A Sunday School class was studying the Ten Commandments. The children were ready to discuss the last one. The teacher asked if anyone could tell her what it was. Susie raised her hand, stood tall and quoted, "Thou shall not take the covers off the neighbor's wife."

*A laugh, to be joyous, must flow from a joyous heart,*
*for without kindness, there can be no true joy.*

—Thomas Carlyle

## IS IT REAL OR "ASSISTED"?

With things like falls, hair extensions, weaves and wigs, you really don't know what is real and what is "assisted hair." Women often try to play the guessing game with one another—come on, tell the truth, "Is that all her hair?" Sometimes you can tell; sometimes you can't. Well, in our ministry we give it away. We are a very lively people—we enjoy getting into the service with the clapping of our hands; singing with a loud voice; dancing, leaping and jumping with exuberant praise.

Oftentimes the women are so enthusiastic about their praise that a ponytail will slip off, a weave extension will come loose and hit the floor. You try to be polite and either look away as if you hadn't seen it or point out to the person that her hair is on the floor. Either way the situation is funny yet uncomfortable for everyone involved.

Well, one Sunday, we were in an uplifting, lively, high-spirited praise. The music was electrifying; the people were dancing, clapping, leaping, shouting and singing. I mean this went on well over ten minutes. That afternoon we had a visiting church fellowship with us. There was one particular guest who was well dressed with a beautiful hairdo, stunning in look. I can only speculate that she must have been overwhelmed by the presence of the Spirit of God through the music and the liberty in our church and just by the way she responded. She danced and leapt and enthusiastically praised God until the sweat beaded on her forehead and ran down the sides of her face. She was so caught up in what she was doing that when she finished praising, she sat down exhausted, reached up to her head, snatched her wig off and used it as a fan.

Never in my life had I witnessed anything like that. Well, at that moment we didn't have to guess if it was real or "assisted" hair.

**Pastor Sharon R. Robinson** leads New Jerusalem Temple of the Living God in Camden, New Jersey.

The Bible says: *Let them praise his name in the dance: let them sing praises unto him with the timbrel and harp.* (Psalm 149:3)

## Reflection

If you've ever gone to a Pentecostal church, on any given day, you can expect to see at least one person shout. But what I love is the unrestrained desire to praise God: No matter what people may say and no matter what people may think, I'm going to praise God anyhow. I love God so much I'm going to do like it says in Psalm 149, ". . . praise His name in the dance." When we can get to a place where we truly fall into the presence of the Lord, we won't care what happens during our praise—even if our hair falls off.

*He who has achieved success has worked well, laughed
often and loved much.*

—Elbert Hubbard

## CATS IN THE PULPIT

It was a typical Sunday morning in a small church that was
in need of many renovations. That's pretty common in churches,
since so many were birthed years and years ago. In this particular church, the ceiling was made of rectangular sections of
cardboard. Don't ask.

On this Sunday morning, it was Family and Friends Day,
and the pastor was in full swing impressing the visitors. In the
pulpit, he was preaching with all his might, sweating and proclaiming the Word of the Lord. All of a sudden, there was a
slight rumble across the ceiling and without warning a cat fell
to the floor. The congregants gasped in shock, and before they
could get out their next breath, lo and behold, in a downward
flight was a second cat. Shock ran through the pews of the
church as the two cats bounced up from the floor and then ran
down the aisle, directly into the vestibule. (Clearly, they knew
of a special exit.)

Well, the excitement wasn't over, for all of a sudden, here
came cat number three. Apparently not everyone was scared
or shocked by this time because one of the bold babies ran into

the aisle and attempted to catch the third cat by the tail. At the tender age of five, this young man wanted to take hold of the situation. The women were adorned in their crystal costume jewelry, and array of suits, some purple, others red, all trimmed in either fur or animal print. These ladies forgot their elegance and immediately screamed and jumped onto the pews, securing themselves by latching on to the shoulders of anyone left sitting!

As the congregants began to return their focus on the pulpit, the pastor had turned his back to them and all that could be seen was the back of the pastor's robe and head with his shoulders bouncing up and down from his laughter. Oh happy days, ohhh the happy days!

**Sheila Jones** is an anointed woman of God and oversees the Drama Ministry, among other things, at Shiloh Pentecostal Church, Inc.—Christian Love Center in Somerville, New Jersey.

The Bible says: *Therefore be ye also ready: for in such an hour as ye think not the Son of man cometh.* (Matthew 24:24)

## Reflection

As hilarious as this story is and unexpected, there is a scripture that admonishes us to "be ye also ready: for in such an hour as ye think not the Son of man cometh." As those church members were sitting in their pews in the beautiful suits and button-down shirts, they were not prepared for the unexpected. No one could have predicted that on that particular Sunday morning cats would start flying from the ceiling. Such is it with those believers who are expecting the return of Jesus Christ. How are you preparing for Christ's arrival? Are you sitting in a pew wearing your finest jewelry but harboring bitterness in your heart? Are you saying one thing and living another? Do you spread the good news of the Gospel? Is your life holy and separated unto God? Just like those cats came out of nowhere, on that Great Day when the Lord cracks the sky—no one will be expecting it . . . for He will come "like a thief in the night." Will you be ready or will you be left behind?

*You cannot hold back a good laugh any more than you can the tide. Both are forces of nature.*

—William Rotsler

## SCOOPING UP THE TRASH

Pastor Robert Schuller states that his yard had lots of work done to it. A crazy mixture of soil and concrete littered his front yard. The workers had left the mess feeling that he could handle the cleanup himself. Pastor Schuller grabbed his rake, broom and plastic bags and went outside to do the work of ten men that would have taken them two days.

As he began to sweep up, his neighbor came out and, with a slight snicker to his mouth, asked Pastor Schuller what he was doing. Pastor Schuller said he was going to clean up the mess the workers left in the yard. Seeing the workload that lay before the good pastor, the neighbor quipped how he'd never get it done. Robert rebutted by having a positive attitude.

The neighbor left. No sooner than just a few minutes after his departure a large dump truck came down the street. It was one of Pastor Schuller's members. The member, happy to see that he was actually driving past the pastor's house, stopped to chat. Pastor Schuller explained his dilemma. Fortunately the dump truck was equipped with all of these special instruments and tools for cleaning up such a mess. It took the church member/dump truck operator one hour to completely clean up the mess. They hugged and departed with promises to see each other at church on Sunday.

However, the dump truck–driving church member left a little bit of rubble, just enough for Pastor Schuller to grab a broom and dispose of it. Just as he was scooping the leftover refuse into the last of about twenty giant plastic bags, the neighbor reappeared. Apparently stunned to see Pastor Schuller scooping up the last of the trash in just over sixty minutes, the neighbor stood bewildered for a few minutes and then asked Pastor Schuller, "What time is service on Sunday?"

**Pastor Robert Harold Schuller** is an American televangelist and pastor known around the world through his weekly *Hour of Power* television program. His Crystal Cathedral in Garden Grove, California, is world renowned for being able to accommodate those in their cars, much like a drive-in theater. He is also the author of over sixty books.

The Bible says: *And when Jesus saw that he became very sorrowful, He said, "How hard it is for those who have riches to enter the kingdom of God! For it is easier for a camel to go through the eye of a needle than for a rich man to enter the kingdom of God." And those who heard it said, "Who then can be saved?" But He said, "The things which are impossible with men are possible with God." Then Peter said, "See, we have left all and followed You."* (Luke 18:24–28, NIV)

## Reflection

The previous story shows how a miracle can happen. Not so much God coming in and doing the impossible, but the miracle in our everyday lives can make the difference. Pastor Schuller's next-door neighbor probably was being daily won over by love and kindness. It wouldn't be completely reasonable to believe that he went to church simply because the yard was cleaned. A positive attitude in the Lord goes a long way in cleaning up the mess.

# Laugh Stop

### Sixteen

A little boy was attending his first wedding. After the service, his cousin asked him, "How many women can a man marry?" "Sixteen," the boy responded. His cousin was amazed that he had an answer so quickly. "How do you know that?" "Easy," the little boy said. "All you have to do is add it up, like the Bishop said: four better, four worse, four richer, four poorer."

### Answering the Call

After a church service on Sunday morning, a young boy suddenly announced to his mother, "Mom, I've decided to become a minister when I grow up." "That's okay with us, but what made you decide that?" "Well," said the little boy, "I have to go to church on Sunday anyway, and I figure it will be more fun to stand up and yell than to sit and listen."

### Trash Passes

A six-year-old was overheard reciting the Lord's Prayer at a church service: "And forgive us our trash passes, as we forgive those who passed trash against us."

### Sermon Notes

A boy was watching his father, a pastor, write a sermon. "How do you know what to say?" he asked. "Why, God tells me." "Oh, then why do you keep crossing things out?"

*Laughter is a powerful way to tap positive emotions.*

—Norman Cousins

## YOU DO?

The late Apostle Arturo Skinner, of the Deliverance Revival Tabernacle Churches, was a man of God who had a great healing and deliverance ministry. The Lord also used him to discern many people's conditions. This, of course, would alert many to believe a miracle was truly about to take place as his revealing of a secret condition led them to acknowledge God was working. After all, how could he have known of a specific sickness or problem?

Back in the early seventies, before the megachurch era that we're currently in, thousands would attend these revivals and crusades of healers and those that operated in the prophetic ministry. At such a crusade at Madison Square Garden in New York City, the Apostle Skinner called a woman out to tell her about her condition. In a manner familiar to many involved in this type of ministry, he spoke to her as if it was her talking. He said to the woman, "I suffer in the lower part of my stomach, isn't that right?" The woman answered, "You do?"

**Pastor Gilbert White** is the senior pastor of God in Action Church in Newark, New Jersey, and has a strong love for young people.

The Bible says: *Having said this, he spit on the ground, made some mud with the saliva, and put it on the man's eyes. "Go," he told him, "wash in the Pool of Siloam" [this word means Sent]. So the man went and washed, and came home seeing.* (John 9:6–7)

## Reflection

One of the biggest mistakes made in the world of theology is to limit God to only the things He typically does. When something arises that seems to be outside the boundaries of His usual practices, we tend to immediately dismiss the actions. Skepticism can have a stunting effect on the good things that God wants to do for His children. Imagine if the man in the scripture above had been appalled at the idea of having mud and spit placed onto his eyes. Today many believers have placed limitations on God and have labeled such actions as absurd. At the same time those who have benefited must wonder about the absurdity of passing up a healing.

# Humor in the Bible

## Humor in Job

Interestingly, the book in the Bible that appears to offer some stinging, yet laughable sarcasm is the book of Job. Considered one of the more somber books of the Bible, its wit comes from an unlikely source, Job himself, and is a bit of a surprise. The book is also one of the few times that it appears God Himself is offering a learning experience in the guise of sarcasm.

Many theologians and scholars also consider it the Bible's actual oldest book, as it contains no explicit Semitic references and its style tends to predate how the law was written.

As stated, it is considered a very somber book. The book is altogether linear in its plot. Job, a successful family man and cattle rancher, is devastated by the complete loss of everything valuable in his life—except for his wife and friends, who, in turn, only offer continued remorse as an answer to his pain. Frustrated, Job strikes back at their intelligence.

The Bible says: *Then Job replied: "Doubtless you are the people, and wisdom will die with you!"* (Job 12:1–2, NIV)

You da man! It's funny how these ancient biblical texts can seemingly take on the vernacular of our modern-day society. It almost seems as if Job is saying in a very sarcastic manner, "You da man and when you die there won't be any wisdom and no one smart left." His sarcasm in regards to their knowledge is again evident in Job 13:5.

The Bible says: *"If only you would be altogether silent! For you, that would be wisdom."* (NIV)

Here again is that twenty-first-century wit. "You know, you're smartest when you're shutting up." Most of us only wish we could get away with such biting responses. Sometimes the smartest thing we could do is to simply shut up. It may not be the kindest thing to say to someone, but it will most definitely spare many a big mouth deeper despair if allowed to continue unabated.

In Chapter 38 of the book of Job, we have our distraught victim expressing his remorse about his situation. God gives Job a bit of his own medicine and poses a stream of difficult queries to his discouraged servant.

The Bible says: *"Where were you when I laid the earth's foundation? Have you ever given orders to the morning, or shown the dawn its place? Have you comprehended the vast expanses of the earth?" "Surely you know, for you were already born! You have lived so many years!"* (Job 38, NIV)

God's response is similar to a parent advising his or her child only to constantly be rebutted with the child's juvenile answers. In exasperation the adult may say, "Well, seeing as you've gotten tons of experience in these matters, maybe I should just let you do all of the talking."

### Sons of Thunder

In the Gospels we find Jesus giving the sons of Zebedee, John and James, the nickname Boanerges, which is translated as Sons of Thunder. Jesus gives them this name as an apparent little tease for what many would consider their personality traits as hotheads. Of all the passages where Jesus speaks, it's the only one where there is an obvious attempt at humor by Jesus.

Here are a few examples of their quick temper and why Jesus gave them this nickname:

The Bible says: *"Teacher," said John, "we saw a man driving out demons in your name and we told him to stop, because he was not one of us." "Do not stop him," Jesus said. "No one who does a miracle in my name can in the next moment say anything bad about me, for whoever is not against us is for us."* (Mark 9:38–40, NIV)

This passage better illustrates their zeal:

The Bible says: *Then the mother of Zebedee's sons came to Jesus with her sons and, kneeling down, asked a favor of him. "What is it you want?" he asked. She said, "Grant that one of these two sons of mine may sit at your right and the other at your left in your kingdom." "You don't know what you are asking," Jesus said to them. "Can you drink the cup I am going to drink?" "We can," they answered. Jesus said to them, "You will indeed drink from my cup, but to sit at my right or left is not for me to grant. These places belong to those for whom they have been prepared by my Father." When the ten heard about this, they were indignant with the two brothers.* (Matthew 20:20–27, NIV)

This may be the passage where Jesus specifically got the idea:

The Bible says: *As the time approached for him to be taken up to heaven, Jesus resolutely set out for Jerusalem. And he sent messengers on ahead, who went into a Samaritan village to get things ready for him; but the people there did not welcome him, because he was heading for Jerusalem. When the disciples James and John saw this, they asked, "Lord, do you want us to call fire down from heaven to destroy them?" But Jesus turned and rebuked them, and they went to another village.* (Luke 9:51–56, NIV)

As a side note, James is the first of the apostles to be killed. John was arrested on numerous occasions and supposedly withstood persecutions.

Here is the passage where Jesus specifically names them Sons of Thunder (another possible rendering is "Sons of Trouble," which of course could have led to the inevitable "Double Trouble" tag):

The Bible says: *James son of Zebedee and his brother John (to them he gave the name Boanerges, which means Sons of Thunder).* (Mark 3:17, NIV)

This kind of light teasing is as common in our modern world as it was in theirs. We might nickname the office worker who treats her coworkers to lunch "Big Time." We might nickname the church worker who hurriedly goes to pick up other congregants "Speedy." In this particular case, these disciples known for their fiery personas are called Sons of Thunder.

# CHAPTER THREE

## Hope Still Remains

*To love means loving the unlovable.*
*To forgive means pardoning the unpardonable.*
*Faith means believing the unbelievable.*
*Hope means hoping when everything seems*
*hopeless.*

—Gilbert Keith Chesterton

One of the more depressing passages in the Bible is Naomi's statement of hopelessness to Ruth. Ruth had wanted to accompany her back home. Naomi was looking at her circumstances in one way and forgetting that God had another blessing. That blessing would only be realized if Ruth and Naomi stayed together.

The Bible says: *But Naomi said, "Return home, my daughters. Why would you come with me? Am I going to have any more sons, who could become your husbands? Return home, my daughters; I am too old to have another husband. Even if I thought there was still hope for me—even if I had a husband tonight and then gave birth to sons—would you wait until they grew up? Would you remain unmarried for them? No, my daughters. It is more bitter for me than for you, because the Lord's hand has gone out against me!"* (Ruth 1:11–13, NIV)

In our world today, we have lost the true meaning and spirit of hope. Today when we use the word "hope," our intentions are really of a "hopelessness." When someone says, "I hope you don't get lost going to the store," he or she is in fact saying that person probably won't return. If someone says your brother will have a successful operation, our response is, "I sure hope so." In these examples, hope is already present. If it's possible under God's strength, then there is still hope.

I'm a believer in hope. My grandfather used to say, "Where there is life, there is hope!" I reflect on that statement often. Hope does still remain, even if you don't think so. Look beyond the hills and see the hope of Glory who sits high above every mountain you will ever face. Hope—it's a word that should always be in our vocabulary. Remember, there is hope that cancer will be cured. There is hope of world peace and an end to war. There is hope that people will really live as one. There is still hope for Martin Luther King's dream to be realized. While we may disregard much of this talk as fanciful, let's not forget that there were millions of black slaves who had hope of freedom. Millions of polio victims who had hope for a cure. Millions of women who fought for the right to vote. All of their hope was not extinguished and neither should yours.

*The soul should always stand ajar, ready to welcome the ecstatic experience.*

—Emily Dickinson

## IT'S FRIDAY, BUT SUNDAY'S COMING

Tony Campolo recalls an epic sermon he heard one Good Friday. There were several ministers speaking. Each one was probably trying to outdo the others with words of wit and tip-top theology. Eventually an elderly minister made his way to the pulpit, where he gave a simple message. The sermon was framed around the line "It's Friday but Sunday's coming!"

"It was Friday; it was Friday and my Jesus was dead on the cross. But that was Friday and Sunday's comin'!

"It was Friday and Mary was cryin' her eyes out. The disciples were runnin' in every direction, like sheep without a shepherd, but that was Friday. Sunday's comin'!" And so the sermon continued, building in volume and power.

"It was Friday. The cynics were lookin' at the world and sayin' you can't change anything. But those cynics didn't know it was Friday. Sunday's comin'!"

Tony recorded that sermon, and as the congregation reached such an excitement level when the preacher delivered the final "It's Friday!" the whole congregation roared back, "BUT SUNDAY'S COMIN'!"

Immediately compiling all the notes from that elderly preacher's message, Tony Campolo wrote one of his most successful books. Of course, it was entitled, *It's Friday, but Sunday's Coming.*

**Anthony "Tony" Campolo** is a well-known pastor, author and public speaker. He has also written over thirty books. He has spent many years as a professor at Eastern College in St. Davids, Pennsylvania.

The Bible says: *But I fear, lest somehow, as the serpent deceived Eve by his craftiness, so your minds may be corrupted from the simplicity that is in Christ.* (2 Corinthians 11:3, NIV)

## Reflection

We can imagine all the dignitaries of the world and the lifestyles they live. What a wonder it must be to go to the places they go and experience the things they do. The food they eat must be indescribable. After so much opulence, what more could they possibly want? The answer for many would be the simple things in life. Once the things that we treasured so much become the mundane, then those things that are truly important to us become the most treasured.

*The only thing you take with you when you're gone is
what you leave behind.*

—John Allston

## ASHES TO ASHES

During one of our recent Sunday services, I'm not sure
why, but one of my members decided to take her shoes off.
This is not as unusual as it sounds, as church folk have been
wearing the wrong size shoes for a long time. It is no great
secret that from time to time they feel the need to release their
soles from their bondage. However, they do tend to put them
back on.

For whatever reason, a woman in my congregation removed
her shoes and did not put them back on when walking around
the church. That's not so bad either. However, she had so much
powder in her shoes she left footprints all over the church. Obviously she was more concerned about leaving the possible . . .
sweet savor . . . of her soles behind rather than the powder. I
can't for the life of me understand how she could have not
looked down and seen the imprint she was leaving.

I should have told her that I am still just a man and that she
doesn't have to remove her shoes because of Holy ground.

**Apostle Joel Rudolph** is the senior pastor of Christian Fellowship Center in Paterson, New Jersey.

The Bible says: *For we brought nothing into the world, and we can take nothing out of it.* (1 Timothy 6:7, NIV)

## Reflection

As we approach the more advanced years in our life, it is not uncommon for us to reflect upon what real contribution we will leave behind.

*The man with an experience is not at the mercy of a man with an argument.*

—Author Unknown

## HITTING THE MARK

A famous preacher of old, Charles Spurgeon, said, "When you preach the Gospel, people should either get mad or get converted." It's a good way to know you're hitting the mark.

**Charles Haddon Spurgeon** (1834–1892) was a British Reformed Baptist preacher who remains highly influential among Christians of different denominations. He wrote many books that have come down to us as complete study guides for the scriptures.

The Bible says: *You stiff-necked and uncircumcised in heart and ears! You always resist the Holy Spirit; as your fathers did, so do you. Which of the prophets did your fathers not persecute? And they killed those who foretold the coming of the Just One, of whom you now have become the betrayers and murderers, who have received the law by the direction of angels and have not kept it." When they heard these things they were cut to the heart, and they gnashed at him with their teeth. But he, being full of the*

*Holy Spirit, gazed into heaven and saw the glory of God, and Jesus standing at the right hand of God, and said, "Look! I see the heavens opened and the Son of Man standing at the right hand of God!" Then they cried out with a loud voice, stopped their ears, and ran at him with one accord; and they cast him out of the city and stoned him.* (Acts 7:51–58a, NIV)

## Reflection

Oftentimes we try to polish up those difficult things that we have to say to someone. In all honesty it is absolutely necessary to present things in an easy-to-receive manner. However, it's those times when there is no easy way to tell someone that one more drink will kill them. To tell your teenaged daughter that the guy she adores is not right. It's those times where the straight truth hurts. It can cause us to be angry with the messenger. At times the messenger could be at fault in his or her delivery. Wouldn't our lives be better if we could just listen to the message?

# Laugh Stop

### Pay to Leave

A little girl became restless as the preacher's sermon dragged on and on. Finally, she leaned over to her mother and whispered, "Mommy, if we give him the money now, will he let us go?"

### Staying Home

After the christening of his baby brother in church, little Johnny sobbed all the way home in the backseat of the car. His father asked him three times what was wrong. Finally, the boy replied, "That priest said he wanted us brought up in a Christian home, and I want to stay with you guys!"

### Pontius the Pilot

Terri asked her Sunday School students to draw pictures of their favorite Bible stories. She was puzzled by Kyle's picture, which showed four people on an airplane, so she asked him which story it was meant to represent. The flight to Egypt was his reply. Pointing at each figure, Ms. Terri said, "That must be Mary, Joseph and Baby Jesus. But who is the fourth person?" "Oh, that's Pontius—the pilot."

### Mommy's a Good Cook

The Sunday School teacher asks, "Now, Johnny, tell me, do you say prayers before eating?" "No sir," little Johnny replies, "I don't have to. My mom is a good cook."

*You cannot be lost on a road that is straight.*

—Author Unknown

## DIRECTIONS

Reverend Billy Graham tells of a time early in his ministry when he arrived in a small town to preach a sermon. Wanting to mail a letter, he asked a young boy where the post office was. When the boy had told him, Dr. Graham thanked him and said, "If you'll come to the Baptist Church this evening, you can hear me telling everyone how to get to heaven." "I don't think I'll be there," the boy said. "You don't even know your way to the post office."

**William Franklin Graham, Jr.** (better known as Billy Graham) is an evangelist and spiritual adviser to multiple U.S. presidents. He is a member of the Southern Baptist Convention. Graham has preached in person to more people around the world than anyone who has ever lived. As of 1993, more than 2.5 million people had stepped forward at his crusades to "accept Jesus Christ as their personal saviour." As of 2002, Graham's lifetime audience, including radio and television broadcasts, topped 2 billion. He is also the author of multiple best-selling books.

The Bible says: *The wolf also shall dwell with the lamb, The leopard shall lie down with the young goat, The calf and the young lion and the fatling together; And a little child shall lead them.* (Isaiah 11:6, NIV)

## Reflection

Face it. It's tough for men to ask for directions. Pride may be the major deterrent in admitting one is lost. The horror of having to ask someone for directions may just be too much. But what do we do about the direction of our lives? The direction that our lives take is based on our choices and our desires. When it comes to good versus evil, we have the right to choose each day the way we will go. We need to seek directions of God in every area of our life if we want to live a Holy life, dedicated and committed to Him. The only requirement to gain God's grace and mercy is that we follow His directions. It's easy—all you have to do is ask Him, for the Bible says, "Seek and ye shall find, knock and the door shall be opened." And in His love for us, God left us the only directional map we will ever need—His Holy Word.

" 'Miracles have ceased.' Have they indeed? When?
*They had not ceased this afternoon when I walked into*
*the wood and got into bright, miraculous sunshine, in*
*shelter from the roaring wind."*

—Ralph Waldo Emerson

## TOTALLY AWESOME

Pastor Charles "Chuck" Swindoll wrote of a kindergarten teacher in a Christian school who was determining how much religious training her new students had. While talking with one little boy, to whom the story of Jesus was obviously brand new, she began relating His death on the cross. When asked what a cross was, she picked up some sticks, and fashioning a crude one, she explained that Jesus was actually nailed to that cross, and then He died. The little boy, with eyes downcast, quietly acknowledged, "Oh, that's too bad." In the very next breath, however, the teacher related that He arose again and that He came back to life. The boy's little eyes got big as saucers. He lit up and exclaimed, "Totally awesome!"

**Pastor Charles "Chuck" Swindoll** is a pastor, an author, an educator and a radio preacher. He founded Insight for Living, currently headquartered in Plano, Texas, which airs a radio program of the same name on more than two thousand stations around the world in fifteen languages. He is currently the senior pastor of Stonebriar Community Church in Frisco, Texas.

> The Bible says: *Now Thomas, called the Twin, one of the twelve, was not with them when Jesus came. The other disciples therefore said to him, "We have seen the Lord." So he said to them, "Unless I see in His hands the print of the nails, and put my finger into the print of the nails, and put my hand into His side, I will not believe." And after eight days His disciples were again inside, and Thomas with them. Jesus came, the doors being shut, and stood in the midst, and said, "Peace to you!" Then He said to Thomas, "Reach your finger here, and look at My hands; and reach your hand here, and put it into My side. Do not be unbelieving, but believing." And Thomas answered and said to Him, "My Lord and my God!"* (John 20:24–28, NIV)

## Reflection

The problem with growing up rich is that the things that would overwhelm most of society are pretty mundane to the wealthy. Most of the Christian world that has grown up with the knowledge of a resurrected carpenter are lulled to sleep by the story. Much like the Apostle Thomas and the young boy in the previous story, it should come as a total astonishment to know that history's greatest tragedy became its greatest victory.

*He who establishes his argument by noise and command shows that his reason is weak.*

—Michel de Montaigne

## THE SQUEALING SHOE

During Bible study, it's normally a quiet time as the pastor or teacher expands or opens the floor so some of the members can ask questions or have open discussions. The atmosphere is more subdued. So it's not normal that you get the "Amen's" or "Praise the Lord's" that you would at the Sunday morning service, where people are more exuberant.

So, just imagine on this particular Tuesday night when the pastor was teaching his weekly Bible study lesson. The church was quiet and all were listening intently to what he was saying, including a young sister, a newer member of the church. As she was listening, she felt a little uncomfortable and started to adjust herself in her seat. As she adjusted herself, the heel of her shoe brushed against the bare floor. The sound, a familiar but normally private one, made everyone slowly lean away from her with bowed heads while holding back smirks.

I'm sure she didn't understand why this was happening, as all she did was scrape the floor with her shoe. Well, it was revealed soon enough when the pastor suggested that she feel free to excuse herself if she needed to go to the bathroom. "Wow!" she must have thought. "Does the pastor and the membership REALLY think I passed gas?" She immediately insisted that she had not passed gas and that it was the heel of her shoe. The pastor, who was failing to contain his laughter, tilted his head to the side and said, "Sure it was, sure," and proceeded to laugh. All the while, this sister was trying to convince the entire Bible study class that it was her shoe!

**Sheila Jones** is an anointed woman of God and oversees the Drama Ministry, among other things, at Shiloh Pentecostal Church, Inc.-Christian Love Center in Somerville, New Jersey.

The Bible says: *May my prayer be set before you like incense; may the lifting up of my hands be like the evening sacrifice. Set a guard over my mouth, O LORD; keep watch over the door of my lips. Let not my heart be drawn to what is evil, to take part in wicked deeds with men who are evildoers; let me not eat of their delicacies.* (Psalm 121:2–4)

## Reflection

It's so simple to assume. It's so easy to make a wrong conjecture. It's so easy to offend someone by what we say—never knowing how this may affect that person later. Although funny in nature, what would have happened if this sister of Zion got offended and ended up leaving the church because of an assumption? Believe it or not, and I'm sure you know it to be true, many people wear their emotions on their sleeve and we have to be careful that what we say, albeit funny, does not offend or cause someone to lose his or her way. Ephesians 5:4 teaches us about "foolish-talking, nor jesting," and how we should be careful even when joking around. Be careful what you say, guard your words, and if you do pass gas, own up to it, spray some Lysol and move on!

# Laugh Stop

### Elijah the Prophet and Gravy Maker

The Sunday School teacher was carefully explaining the story of Elijah the Prophet and the false prophets of Baal. She explained how Elijah built the altar, put wood upon it, cut the steer in pieces and laid it upon the altar.

And then Elijah commanded the people of God to fill four barrels of water and pour it over the altar. He had them do this four times.

"Now," said the teacher, "can anyone in the class tell me why the Lord would have Elijah pour water over the steer on the altar?" A little girl in the back of the room started waving her hand. "I know, I know," she said. "To make the gravy!"

### Traveling Salesman

Our parish priest was making a visit to my nephew's home. He knocked on the door, and the little four-year-old boy went to the door and saw the priest. He called to his dad, "Hey, Dad! That guy that works for God is here!"

### Lot and the Telephone Pole

The Sunday School teacher had just finished the lesson. She had taught the portion of the Bible that told of how Lot's wife looked back and turned into a pillar of salt. She then asked if anyone had any questions or comments. A little boy raised his hand and said, "My mommy looked back once when she was driving and she turned into a telephone pole!"

*If it is sanity you are after, there is no recipe like laughter.*

—Henry Elliot

## THE GREEN-EYED MONSTER

Contained in the Bible, there are many examples of Jesus casting out demons, and over the years, there have been many movies that have exemplified the presence of demonic forces: *The Exorcist, The Omen, Rosemary's Baby*. So it's no surprise that demonic forces sometimes find their way into the church.

Not long ago, a young man came to the altar at church and was just learning about the ways of God and was literally battling between good and evil. A missionary, under the power of the Holy Spirit, looked at the man and immediately saw that there were demonic forces attached to him. So all of a sudden, the missionary started speaking and said, "Come out, come out, you green-eyed monster. Come out of him, I say!"

The man said, still not being completely delivered, "Let me help you. Come out, you [blankety blank] demon. Come out, you [blankety blank] demon." Suffice it to say, the missionary stopped talking.

Author unknown.

The Bible says: *While they were going out, a man who was demon-possessed and could not talk was brought to Jesus. And when the demon was driven out, the man who had been mute spoke. The crowd was amazed and said, "Nothing like this has ever been seen in Israel."* (Matthew 9:32–33)

## Reflection

I'm sure the missionary wished she could have muted what the man at the altar was saying. However, we are entangled in a world where good is constantly confronted by evil. Although this may cause consternation with many who are good, it is the opinion of many that the real evil is when the good decide not to confront evil things.

*When I held you in my arms at your baptism, I wanted it to be a fresh start for you to be more complete than we had ever been ourselves, but I wonder if we expected too much.*

—Richard Olton

## THE BAPTISM TWIST

As a ten-year-old, I was touched in my heart to get baptized. This took place in North Carolina in the summer of 1973. Because I was an only child, my parents would pack my bags and ship me to my grandmother's the day after school closed for summer recess. I would be brought back a few days before school started. I'm sure this was as much a break for them as it was for me. I personally hated going down there for the summer, as all my friends were up here.

Back during those days there were fewer accommodations for a ten-year-old in North Carolina than there might be today. There were a total of only three TV stations in the area. My grandmother lived, what seemed like, one hundred miles from the nearest neighborhood. Some of the conveniences that were missed were things like a phone, a bathroom, running indoor water and getting a haircut. This was back in the days of the big Afro and I was a slave to fashion. It would only worsen, however, as there were few barbers in that area. So my Afro would grow to mammoth proportions until I could get back to civilization in New Jersey.

One of the things I hated most was my grandmother's insane drive to attend every single church meeting that came down the pike, and when there was a revival in town, then that was the worst. Every single night we attended church. Didn't she know the Osmonds were coming on? Well, wouldn't you know it? One of those nights a spark hit me and I decided to get baptized. Arrangements were made for me to get my dunking on the day that had been set aside for everyone to get baptized.

This was late in the summer and my fast-growing Afro had reached about twelve inches. I can remember using a neighbor's phone and telling my mom and dad. My mom told me that my dad had gone out on the porch and was crying. At that time I couldn't have imagined why.

Well, anyway, the associate ministers led me into the baptismal pool with my long Afro. The minister put his huge hand on top of my head and dipped this city kid, who hated being under water, into the pool. I survived, but when I came out of the pool, there was a surprise for everyone. I began to shake my head vigorously with my long hair and the ministers went for cover. I probably resembled a black sheepdog. Of course, all of this was unknown to me, but it was relayed to me later by my grandmother. Probably the next kid with a huge Afro was made to wear a shower cap.

**Randy Vaughan** is an author and a member of Shiloh Pentecostal Church, Inc.–Christian Love Center in Somerville, New Jersey.

The Bible says: *Then they spoke the word of the Lord to him and to all the others in his house. At that hour of the night the jailer took them and washed their wounds; then immediately he and all his family were baptized. The jailer brought them into his house and set a meal before them; he was filled with joy because he had come to believe in God— he and his whole family.* (Acts 16:32–34, NIV)

## Reflection

The book of Isaiah talks about a child leading them. This is meant as an obvious contradiction to the fact that normally children are to be led. The wonderful thing about leading children is that they are more led by example than by command. Whether it is a baptism or being a good spouse, a leader in the church or community or lastly a parent, the primary teaching aid is and will always be not what you know, but what you show.

*The old Irish when immersing a babe at baptism left
out the right arm so that it would remain pagan for
good fighting.*

—Anonymous

## TAKE ME TO THE WATER—AGAIN!

Baptism by water submersion is a never-ending occurrence
in the Christian church. In Acts 2:38 the Bible teaches us to
"repent and be baptized." His cousin, John the Baptist, baptized Jesus himself. Deacon Philip baptized the eunuch in water
after he ministered to him. The Apostle Paul, although not one
to brag about his baptisms, also continued the ritual by bap-
tizing the jailer's family as well as a few in the city of Corinth.
I also follow the examples set forth by Jesus Christ by contin-
uing to baptize those believers who have come to accept Jesus
Christ as their Lord and Savior.

On this particular Sunday, as I was preparing for baptisms,
I noticed, however, that the water in the baptismal pool was extremely cold. The first candidate for baptism, a woman, started
walking to the water to be baptized. To be positive about her
decision, I informed her that the water was really cold and that
she could wait to be baptized at a later date when the water
was warmer. Feeling that this was the time God wanted her to
make the right steps in her life, she insisted that she be bap-

tized right then and there. Not thinking she heard me correctly, I asked again, "Are you sure?" Shaking her head in the affirmative, she said, "Yes."

So I obliged and assisted her as she continued walking to the water and immediately she started muttering, "Oh Jesus! Oh Jesus!" She moved closer to the water and her groans got louder, "OH Jesus! OH Jesus!" As she now started stepping into the water, she said even louder, "OH JESUS! OH JESUS! OH JESUS!" Feeling that this was not the time for a long message, I quickly read the scripture and pronounced, "I now baptize you in the name of Jesus Christ!" As she got immersed fully into the water, she quickly jumped up and stated, "Oh SH**, that water was cold!" The deacon on duty immediately yelled, "Pastor, dip her again; it didn't take!"

Maybe it would have been warmer the second time around.

**Dr. Creflo A. Dollar** is the senior pastor of World Changers Church International with churches in College Park, Georgia; New York City; and Battle Creek, Michigan. His daily broadcast, *Changing Your World*, can be seen in most countries around the world. More than thirty thousand members enter the doors of World Changers on any given Sunday. He is also the author of several best-selling books on living better lives and increasing our faith.

The Bible says: *And this water symbolizes baptism that now saves you also—not the removal of dirt from the body but the pledge of a good conscience toward God.* (1 Peter 3:21, NIV)

## Reflection

How many times do we wish we could take back what we said—probably every day. Even when you have the best intentions, sometimes our mouths just seem to get us in trouble. Thank God, He knows our hearts and our every intention. Although the sister slipped immediately after she was baptized, I believe that God knew her heart and His grace covered her even then. You see, we all fail. That's just a part of our life. No matter what we say or do, there is none who is perfect, no one. The pressures of life can make us do and say things we really don't want to say—for it's not what goes into a person, but what comes out. So be guarded—because it's easy to slip even at the most visible time.

# Humor in the Bible

## Let's Make a Deal, Abraham

Have you ever encountered people who can't make their minds up? Then when given additional options, they continue to get even more indecisive. This is seemingly what occurs with Abraham in this story. God apparently is willing to grant grace to Sodom and Gomorrah, where Abe's nephew Lot lives.

The Bible says: *Then Abraham approached him and said: "Will you sweep away the righteous with the wicked? What if there are fifty righteous people in the city? Will you really sweep it away and not spare the place for the sake of the fifty righteous people in it? Far be it from you to do such a thing—to kill the righteous with the wicked, treating the righteous and the wicked alike. Far be it from you! Will not the Judge of all the earth do right?" The LORD said, "If I find fifty righteous people in the city of Sodom, I will spare the whole place for their sake." Then Abraham spoke up again: "Now that I have been so bold as to speak to the Lord, though I am nothing but dust and ashes, what if the number of the righteous is five less than fifty? Will you destroy the whole city because of five people?" "If I*

*find forty-five there," he said, "I will not destroy it." Once
again he spoke to him, "What if only forty are found there?"
He said, "For the sake of forty, I will not do it." Then he
said, "May the Lord not be angry, but let me speak. What
if only thirty can be found there?" He answered, "I will not
do it if I find thirty there." Abraham said, "Now that I have
been so bold as to speak to the Lord, what if only twenty can
be found there?" He said, "For the sake of twenty, I will not
destroy it." Then he said, "May the Lord not be angry, but
let me speak just once more. What if only ten can be found
there?" He answered, "For the sake of ten, I will not destroy
it." When the LORD had finished speaking with Abraham,
he left, and Abraham returned home.* (Genesis 18:25–33,
NIV)

Can you imagine Abraham going, "Okay . . . no . . . wait a
minute, let's renegotiate." Without intending to sound sacrilegious,
it can even be imagined God speaking to Abraham with a smile
as He accommodated Abe's requests. Unfortunately Abraham
did not go low enough and the citizens of Sodom and Gomorrah
were not spared. The second-guessing and flip-flopping probably reminds most of us of a dinner companion who can't make
his or her mind up when ordering food. If you can't think of
anyone like that, then it's probably you.

## A Funny-Looking Fish

Most things in the Bible that we may find humorous rarely
incite our visual senses. This is not one of those cases. You had
to be there!

The Bible says: *After Jesus and his disciples arrived in Capernaum, the collectors of the two-drachma tax came to Peter and asked, "Doesn't your teacher pay the temple tax?" "Yes, he does," he replied. When Peter came into the house, Jesus was the first to speak. "What do you think, Simon?" he asked. "From whom do the kings of the earth collect duty and taxes—from their own sons or from others?" "From others," Peter answered. "Then the sons are exempt," Jesus said to him. "But so that we may not offend them, go to the lake and throw out your line. Take the first fish you catch; open its mouth and you will find a four-drachma coin. Take it and give it to them for my tax and yours."* (Matthew 17:24–26, NIV)

It would be a hard choice to be excited about getting the money or to bust up laughing with a fish sticking a coin out of his mouth. Most scholars are stuck for the reasoning behind Jesus using this format to assist His disciple Peter in paying his tax bill. It's not a hard thing to surmise that most people receiving a financial blessing in this manner would probably prefer a big fish to hold more money.

To many taxpayers, it could have been a shark. He still would have had to give up the money.

# CHAPTER FOUR

## Holy Ghost Explosion

~⌀~

*But ye shall receive power, after that the Holy*
*Ghost is come upon you: and ye shall be*
*witnesses unto me both in Jerusalem, and in all*
*Judaea, and in Samaria, and unto the uttermost*
*part of the earth.*

—Acts 1:8

Many times, especially in old-school church, we've heard the phrase "Holy Ghost Explosion." What the saying often means is that we would experience the movement of the Spirit of God like it was meant to be experienced—a manifestation of miracles, signs, healings and souls being saved.

Images of the old-fashioned tent revivals often come to mind as a place where the atmosphere was charged with the excitement of the Holy Ghost. A place where long ago worship services would last until the morning hours.

We've seen this move in the book of Acts:

The Bible says: *When the day of Pentecost came, they were all together in one place. Suddenly a sound like the blowing of a violent wind came from heaven and filled the whole house where they were sitting. They saw what seemed to be tongues of fire that separated and came to rest on each of them. All of them were filled with the Holy Spirit and began to speak in other tongues as the Spirit enabled them.* (Acts 2:4, NIV)

Over the years, I have been able to witness Holy Ghost Explosions on several occasions. I've seen the power of God so heavy that people were just falling out everywhere—bowing down to His majesty, crying, leaping, running, shouting and, yes, even laughing. Some of these stories, although funny, remind us how sweet the gift of the Holy Spirit can be and how precious it is that God would send us a comforter that will forever be present with us if we live upright before Him.

*Laughter is a tranquilizer with no side effects.*

—Arnold H. Glasgow

## DO YOU SEE WHAT I SEE?

Have you ever been to a healing service? There are men and women in the body of Christ across the country and in the world who have been anointed with the gift of healing. Healing services are evidenced across the world, and the life of Jesus Christ was a living example of the healing power of God. However, not all the time is this displayed. Many in an attempt to force a miracle have left many in bewilderment and, yes, even laughing.

One such prophet of God was led to have a healing service in New Brunswick, New Jersey. As he was ministering, he was led to ask those who wanted to see or be healed from blindness to come to the altar and receive their healing. Droves of people rose from their seats to make their way to the front of the church, as they were excited to feel the movement of God in their lives. The prophet asked all those who had glasses to put them on the floor and believe in God for a miracle. This is not uncommon in healing services, as many feel they must show an act of faith before the miraculous can happen. As he was praying, all of a sudden, he started stomping on all the glasses that were laid on the floor. The prayers continued, the Amen was said and those who had come to the altar were asked to go back to their seats praising God.

As they made their way back to their seats, some of those who came for healing had to feel their way back because without their glasses they could not see a thing. What a sight to behold (no pun intended)!

**Noel Goring** is a minister of music at Zion Tabernacle of Praise in Piscataway, New Jersey, and First Baptist Church of Lincoln Gardens in New Jersey.

The Bible says: *And when Jesus departed thence, two blind men followed him, crying, and saying, "Thou Son of David, have mercy on us." And when he was come into the house, the blind men came to him: and Jesus saith unto them, "Believe ye that I am able to do this?" They said unto him, "Yeah Lord." Then touch he their eyes, saying, "According to your faith be it unto you."* (Matthew 9:27–29)

*"Cursed is the man who leads the blind astray on the road." Then all the people shall say, "Amen!"* (Deuteronomy 27:18)

### Reflection

Many people may say that the prophet of God who held the healing service missed it. But what many may not have realized is that although the healing power of God was present in the room, the key activator to the people's complete healing was faith to believe that God would and could do it. The woman with the issue of blood (Matthew 9:20–22) is one of the most notable stories in the Bible faith and belief in the healing power of God. Not only did she believe that by touching Jesus's garment she would be healed, but she went against tradition by even leaving her house in what was considered an unclean condition. By faith, however, she knew that one touch would change her life forever. And it did. Do you need healing today? One touch of faith is all you need for God's supernatural healing power to change the course of your life.

*Drop the idea that you are Atlas carrying the world on your shoulders. The world would go on even without you. Don't take yourself so seriously.*

—Norman Vincent Peale

## I NEED A HANKY

During a recent conference where Joyce Meyer was speaking, the stadium was packed. Everyone was hanging on to every word that was coming forth from Joyce. She was walking back and forth across the stage, in her white dress suit, as is her fashion, with her handkerchief swaying to the side.

As she walked and talked, she said, "I can't talk about all this stuff anymore. I can't care about what you think about this service tonight. I'm not responsible for this thing. . . . God's running it."

At that moment, with her hanky in her right hand, she reached up to either scratch or wipe sweat from behind her right ear. As she casually lowered her hand, she realized that the hanky had disappeared. She looked at her right hand and then her left hand momentarily dumbfounded as the audience roared. It was only then that she realized the handkerchief was caught up in her earring. Not able to compose herself, she bowed over in laughter as the worshippers followed suit.

**Joyce Meyer** is a popular Christian author and speaker. Her television and radio programs air in twenty-five languages in two hundred countries, and she has written over seventy books on Christianity.

The Bible says: *But Joseph said to them, "Don't be afraid. Am I in the place of God? You intended to harm me, but God intended it for good to accomplish what is now being done, the saving of many lives. So then, don't be afraid. I will provide for you and your children." And he reassured them and spoke kindly to them.* (Genesis 50:19–21, NIV)

## Reflection

Much like Joseph, Joyce Meyer teaches us an even bigger lesson here than what was intended. That is to be able to laugh at ourselves sometimes. During serious times, when we think there is no room for lightheartedness, it's then that a little levity is even more warranted. It borders on pompousness to think that whatever our task may be it is the most important matter in all the universe. Take the time to enjoy the mistakes, errors and mishaps in life and we may find that the task still gets done.

*Endurance is patience concentrated.*

—Thomas Carlyle

## GOING THE DISTANCE

People were falling out from the Spirit. The church was in a frenzy. However, there were several who had not been carried away with the excitement. They really wanted to experience Jesus, but they wanted a clear mind and not to be caught up with emotions. Eric was among this group on this particular night at this church during a revival. He had made a vow to himself not to be swept away, and that if he were to be called up, it would have to be God who made him fall out from the Spirit and not the visiting minister pushing him down.

Eric was eventually called up and subsequently hands were laid on him. The evangelist continued to push and push, but the young Christian would not yield to the peer pressure to fall out. What a sight it was as the evangelist was trying to push him down and the young man was standing there fighting to stay afoot. His friends could not contain themselves in the charged atmosphere and had to smother their giggles as Eric stood there wobbling, but wouldn't fall.

Eventually out of exhaustion and probably embarrassment, he allowed Eric to go back to his seat unslain. The "catcher" had the weirdest look of bewilderment. Eric had won. He had gone the distance.

Author unknown.

The Bible says: *Then the LORD said to me, "The prophets are prophesying lies in my name. I have not sent them or appointed them or spoken to them. They are prophesying to you false visions, divinations, idolatries and the delusions of their own minds. Therefore, this is what the LORD says about the prophets who are prophesying in my name: I did not send them.* (Jeremiah 14:14–15, NIV)

## Reflection

Seeking after the true experience of God goes beyond the obvious supernatural and miraculous. While many are looking for another Jesus to actually walk on water, they miss the even more important extended hand of His to pull a young man from life on the streets, a woman from childhood abuse and the myriad of everyday miracles He performs. We look for an angel and look past the grocer who allowed you to go for five dollars short. We look for a supernatural healing and are bored when the doctor tells us that we're in good shape. Experiencing God is so much more than the miracle. It's also not allowing ourselves to be pushed, but rather to go the distance.

# *Laugh Stop*

### Take Me Out to the Ball Game

A father took his five-year-old son to several baseball games where "The Star-Spangled Banner" was sung before the start of each game. Then the father and son attended a church on a Sunday shortly before Independence Day. The congregation sang "The Star-Spangled Banner," and after everyone sat down, the little boy suddenly yelled, "PLAY BALL!!!"

### Happy Birthday!

A mother took her three-year-old daughter to church for the first time. The church lights were lowered, and then the choir came down the aisle, carrying lighted candles. All was quiet until the little one started to sing loudly, "Happy Birthday to you. Happy Birthday to you . . ."

### The Whistle Prayer

During the minister's prayer one Sunday, there was a loud whistle from one of the back pews. Gary's mother was horrified. She pinched him into silence and after church asked: "Gary, whatever made you do such a thing?" Gary answered soberly: "I asked God to teach me to whistle . . . and just then, He did!"

*Take the first step in faith. You don't have to see the whole staircase, just take the first step.*

—Martin Luther King, Jr.

## KEEP YOUR HEAD TOGETHER

There was a man whom everyone in the church was familiar with who was up in line for prayer. Well, the pastor was really feeling the Holy Ghost and I noticed that he was laying his hands on top of everyone's head as compared to where he usually does, which is on the forehead. Well, it didn't bother anyone except this particular man because he wore a toupee at the time. I saw the uneasiness in his face when the pastor approached him. I guess I was probably looking for it or it was just the look on his face was too obvious. Well, I guess he felt he didn't actually need that touch or a blessing from the Lord that bad because he was maneuvering his way out of the prayer line and was attempting to bounce. Fortunately the aisle was only four feet wide and it was packed shoulder to shoulder—he couldn't move! Then it happened—the pastor laid a Vulcan hand grip on top of the man's head while the soles of his feet were still trying to find a way to bolt. Now here is where you need to use your spiritual or even your not-so-spiritual imagination. . . .

The pastor had his eyes closed, hand on top of the man's head, swirling his hand around like he was making a red velvet cake, talking to the Lord on behalf of the man. Meanwhile, the man's eyes were wide open (like the deer on I-95 around 2 A.M. staring into your headlights), his hand on top of the pastor's, trying to make sure nothing was snatched off. Now, we have these two grown men engaging in the Hindu-like swirling motion dance, one praying to God for intervention and the other praying that God won't answer (at least until later) so his cover won't be exposed to all.

**Randy Vaughan** is an author and a member of Shiloh Pentecostal Church, Inc.–Christian Love Center in Somerville, New Jersey.

The Bible says: *Then the eyes of both of them were opened, and they realized they were naked; so they sewed fig leaves together and made coverings for themselves.* (Genesis 3:7, NIV)

## Reflection

Isn't it interesting how we sometimes think we've hidden something from our loved ones? Something that we may think is a little embarrassing. The slight imperfection that we somehow feel will make the difference. Then when we find out that all along they knew about our little secret—surprise—they love us anyway. This is the same thing we do with God many times. We refuse to have honest conversation with Him. It's as if we've hidden our secret from His eyes. When we finally relent and let Him into the deeper cavities of our lives, we find His love is still there.

*Regardless of how you feel inside, always try to look like a winner. Even if you are behind, a sustained look of control and confidence can give you a mental edge that results in victory.*

—Arthur Ashe

## SLIPPED UP AND SHOUTED OUT

In many of the churches in our culture, be they Baptist, Methodist, Pentecostal or charismatic, it is not uncommon to see a display of joy or excitement expressed in the form of shouting. The individual standing up and/or dancing joyously typically accompanies this. On one occasion at my church, a woman began shouting and stood up to cut a step. She soon got so caught up in the . . . joy that she shouted right out of her slip. An alert usher, that is, a female usher, came up behind her, shouting right along with her, and from behind pulled her slip up and shouted her right out the door. The women of the church had, in shock, stopped shouting, but it appeared the men had not.

**Apostle Joel Rudolph** is the senior pastor of Christian Fellowship Center in Paterson, New Jersey.

The Bible says: *Once when we were going to the place of prayer, a slave girl who had a spirit by which she pre-*

*dicted the future met us. She earned a great deal of money for her owners by fortune telling. This girl followed Paul and the rest of us, shouting, "These men are servants of the Most High God, who are telling you the way to be saved." She kept this up for many days. Finally Paul became so troubled that he turned around and said to the spirit, "In the name of Jesus Christ I command you to come out of her!" At that moment the spirit left her.* (Acts 16:16–18, NIV)

## Reflection

To beginning Bible students, the above passage in Acts has called many to scratch their head in bewilderment. After all, it appeared that the young girl was being admirable as she appeared to be bolstering Paul's ministry. It soon became apparent her unchecked exuberance was a hindrance not only to him and the community, but to the girl herself. Thankfully Paul was able to rectify the situation swiftly. While we may have the correct destination in mind, we must remember that the traveling there is still a very important part of the arrival.

*What soap is to the body, laughter is to the soul.*

—Yiddish Proverb

## HOLY GHOST MAKEUP

How many can remember a good old-fashioned tarry service? If you've been around the church for a long time, you can remember the days when the old saints would gather everyone around the altar who desired to receive the Holy Spirit. In the old days and still in some Pentecostal churches today, believers will get together with new converts or those wishing to speak in tongues as the Spirit gave utterance. This became known as a tarrying service. The term "tarry" developed from the book of Acts in the New Testament, which simply means "to wait" in modern English. Tarrying eventually came to symbolize those wishing to receive the Holy Spirit (or Ghost, depending on what Bible version you're reading) with the evidence of speaking in other tongues. Those reflecting on the good old days will reminisce as to how long it would take. Unified voices in these Pentecostal churches could be heard saying "Hallelujah, Hallelujah, Hallelujah and Hallelujah" throughout the church as young and old, rich and poor travailed day and night to receive the precious gift that was promised to those who believed in the Lord Jesus Christ. Then in came Sandra.

Sandra was not the typical saint. She wore jewelry and lots of rouge. Sandra also wore loud lipstick. This was not something done in earlier sanctified or Pentecostal churches. According to her church, you had to dress saintly, look holy and have a clean face. Jewelry and makeup were against God. Some would even refer to women who wore excessive makeup, or any for that matter, as Jezebel. Sandra didn't agree. She felt that what people saw didn't matter; it was what God saw that did. So as she slowly walked up to the front of the church desiring to receive the Holy Spirit, you can only imagine how the mood changed. Mouths flew open, hands went out in the air, people backed away from the altar—but Sandra never looked back. All she wanted was a touch from the Holy Spirit. As she lay her face on the altar, an open vessel desiring nothing but a touch from the Lord, the Holy Spirit empowered her and she started speaking in tongues. Imagine the faces of the people. God touched the soul of a woman they considered to be against the things of God. But it was the voice of a young child that probably verbalized all that some of them were thinking when she said, "Mommy, look at that! All anybody has to do is put on some makeup and then they can get the Holy Ghost! Isn't that cool? And oh boy, it will save so much time!" Out of the mouths of babes . . .

The contributor wishes to remain anonymous.

The Bible says: *But the LORD said unto Samuel, Look not on his countenance, or on the height of his stature; be-*

*cause I have refused him: for [the LORD seeth] not as
man seeth; for man looketh on the outward appearance,
but the LORD looketh on the heart.* (I Samuel 16:7)

## Reflection

How many times have we looked at people and made a judgment about who they were? You probably didn't know anything about them but made an assumption based on how they
looked, how they talked, what they had on, how they responded
or what someone else said. The Bible tells us to "judge not, lest
ye be judged." And most of the times when you judge, you get
it all wrong anyway. Most non-Christians consider Christians
the most judgmental people who have ever lived. That should
not be. Just like Samuel when he was told by God to go to the
sons of Jesse and anoint the next king—he looked at the outward appearance, and never thought that the one who was in
the field tending to the sheep would become the king after God's
own heart. It was then that Samuel learned that God does not
see as man sees: He doesn't look on the outward appearance as
we do; He looks on the heart—where we can't see, only God
can. That's why we shouldn't judge—if you do, you'll get a
Holy Ghost Makeup surprise and realize that someone for God
is not based on our definition, but God's.

*If I couldn't laugh, I'd rather die.*

—Claudette Colbert

## WHENEVER YOU'RE READY . . .

One Sunday afternoon service, my bishop had an appointment to preach at another church in the area. Now this particular church has been known to have fake shouting, erroneous doctrine and sudden breakouts of unseasoned saints, sprinting around the sanctuary and pretending to feel the Spirit of God. My bishop happens to be in his nineties so he is old school, and a Holiness-or-nothing type of man. In my mind, knowing what I knew about this church that we're about to visit, I'm like, "They're in for a big surprise" because there will be no compromising of God's Word this day. The pastor of that church greeted his members with a few words, accompanied by song, which resulted in shouting. I personally didn't feel the anointing, so I sat extremely still, as did the members of my church, and so did my bishop. The people in this church were running like track stars in Easter clothes around this sanctuary so fast that I got dizzy trying to focus on just one person. There they were—colorful suits and dresses sprinting and grape killing. Stomping in awkward dance steps consciously fake shouting! Finally, my bishop stood up as if to say enough was enough. I'm on the edge of my seat like, "Here we go." He grabbed a

microphone and signaled for the music to stop. Well, along with
the music, so did all but one of the people who were shouting.
This young man didn't know how to reel in his choreographed
shout. There he was, at the front of the church, and right below
the bishop, doing a rain dance with no music. Not only that,
but the church was as quiet as a library, and everyone was staring at him. The bishop said, "All right, son, you can find your
seat now." Instantly the young man stopped, looked around
and walked back to his seat. You see, his eyes were closed the
whole time so he had no idea that he was the only one jumping up and down for at least ten feet in every direction. It was
so embarrassing that I couldn't even laugh. I thought, "How
does one play that off and act as if it didn't happen?" The
bishop, who is as no nonsense as they come, said, "Y'all got to
stop all that dancing and get to know God." "When you get
the Holy Ghost, you will have power, but not enough to stop
yourself from praising God, whenever you're ready to sit down."

**Shawn Wilkins** is a music pioneer, composer and songwriter. He has written several hit songs for various artists such
as Father MC, Raven Simone and Yo Yo, to name a few.
Shawn is currently working on his first novel, entitled *The Black
Church.*

The Bible says: *"Now the Lord is that Spirit: and where
the Spirit of the Lord [is], there [is] liberty."* (2 Corinthians 3:17, NIV)

## Reflection

Freedom in Christ is a beautiful thing. Free to worship. Free to praise. Free to sing. Free to laugh. Free to experience God in his fullness. Don't take that freedom for granted—it's a priceless commodity and one that will give you a life of peace, joy, happiness, grace and unconditional love.

# *Laugh Stop*

### Our Father . . .

One little girl began her prayer like this: "Our Father, who are in heaven, hello! What be Thy name?" A boy who thought he knew the answer to that question prayed, "Our Father, who art in heaven, Harold be Thy name." The prayer of another boy went like this: "Our Father who art in heaven, Hollywood be Thy name." A girl whose visiting uncle was a horse player bowed her head with a plea that God "give us this day our daily double." A five-year-old girl who was trying to cope with Sunday School and kindergarten at the same time came up with this charming blend of church and state: "Give us this day our daily bread, and liberty and justice for all." Another kinder-gartener asked God to "give us this day our jelly bread." Then there was the little boy who prayed, "Forgive us our dentists, as we forgive our dentists." Another boy pleaded, "Lead us not into creation." Then there was the farmer's boy who said, "De-liver us from weevils." Another boy prayed to God to "deliver us from eagles." And a boy climaxed his prayer like this: "For thine is the kingdom, and the power, and the glory, forever and ever, Amen and F.M." One particular four-year-old prayed, "And forgive us our trash baskets as we forgive those who put trash in our baskets." A three-year-old said, "Our Father, Who does art in heaven, Harold is His name. Amen."

### An Observation

Two kids were walking home from Sunday School, each deep in his own thoughts. Finally one said, "What do you think about all this devil business we studied today?" The other boy replied thoughtfully, "Well, you know how Santa Claus turned out. This is probably just your dad, too. . . ."

*Laughter is the sun that drives winter from the human face.*

—Victor Hugo

## HIGH-PRAISE HAIR

The church was in high praise, the band was at full momentum and the saints were dancing and "shouting" with great liberty. A very proper and delicate sister began to rejoice through dance. She was not the type who we would generalize and think would participate in a spontaneous praise moment. However, something touched her and she proceeded to do the David dance, no holds barred. Slowly her sophisticated hairstyle began to unwind. A few strands here and a few strands there. Once the dance ended, the hairstyle was no more. The entire hairstyle was made of attached hair, which lay breathless on the floor. A polite sister-in-Christ retrieved the hair from the floor and eased it into the dancer's hand as she returned to her seat.

**Sheila Jones** is an anointed woman of God and oversees the Drama Ministry, among other things, at Shiloh Pentecostal Church, Inc.-Christian Love Center in Somerville, New Jersey.

The Bible says: *David, wearing a linen ephod, danced before the LORD with all his might, while he and the en-*

*tire house of Israel brought up the ark of the LORD with shouts and the sound of trumpets. As the ark of the LORD was entering the City of David, Michal daughter of Saul watched from a window. And when she saw King David leaping and dancing before the LORD, she despised him in her heart.* (2 Samuel 6:14–16, NIV)

## Reflection

At the end of the 1970 movie *Beneath the Planet of the Apes*, a sequel to 1968's *The Planet of the Apes*, the humans living with the nuclear bomb took off their fake faces to reveal a less pleasant feature. Prior to doing this, they said, "To our God we reveal our innermost self." Shouldn't we all have this approach to the all-knowing God instead of hiding behind a mask as if He didn't know the real us?

The previous passage, where David dances, typically reflects our opinion of those who do something that may be embarrassing. Usually this shame is more the offspring of an acquaintance rather than those performing such "embarrassing" antics themselves. However, if we take a step back and attempt to understand what joy and honesty it would take for anyone to sacrifice his "dignity" to reveal his innermost self to his God, maybe we would all be a little more willing to do David's dance.

*A laugh is a smile that bursts.*

—Mary H. Waldrip

## HE'S OUT!

Tent revivals. Deliverance services. Azusa experiences. Revival. When those names are attached to a special program or service, it's pretty much a given that the move of God will be experienced in a most miraculous way. Azusa is one of the greatest examples of the power of the Holy Ghost. The Azusa Street Revival was a Pentecostal revival meeting that took place in Los Angeles, California, and was led by William J. Seymour, an African-American preacher. It began with a meeting on April 14, 1906, at the African Methodist Episcopal Church and continued until roughly 1915. The revival was characterized by speaking in tongues, dramatic worship services and interracial mingling. The participants received criticism from secular media and Christian theologians for behaviors considered to be outrageous and unorthodox, especially at the time. Today, the revival is considered by historians have been the primary catalyst for the spread of Pentecostalism in the twentieth century.

The late Apostle Arturo Skinner, of the Deliverance Revival Tabernacle Churches, may not have been at Azusa, but he was world renowned for his God-given gifts of healing and deliverance. Apostle Skinner's faith was so great that he believed God could deliver anyone of anything at any given time—no matter how grave the situation or how far you may have strayed away from the faith.

However, this was one particular service where the one who was looking for deliverance, I guess, felt Apostle Skinner may have needed a little more help. As the story goes, during one of his infamous deliverance services, Apostle Skinner was praying for the deliverance of a man who battled with alcohol. As he was rebuking the spirits, the drunk man stood tall at the altar while Apostle Skinner prayed over him. After a long while, the drunk man started getting tired and finally lifted up the Apostle's hand and said, "He's out, preacher!" No one knows to this day if the man was delivered or just tired of standing.

**Pastor Gilbert White** is the senior pastor of God in Action Church in Newark, New Jersey.

The Bible says: *So then neither is he that planteth any thing, neither he that watereth; but God that giveth the increase.* (I Corinthians 3:7)

## Reflection

I wonder whatever happened to the young man whom Apostle Skinner was praying for. Did he ever get delivered? Is he still struggling with alcohol? I wonder if he's a preacher now. You never know. That's why it's so important to continue to lay the foundation of love and grace and peace to those who may not have a relationship with God. You never know what your example will yield one, two or even five years from now. I had a friend whom I was sharing the Gospel with for years. I would send daily meditations, talk to her about the Word of God, but she never gave me any indication that the message of God's love was sinking in. Until one Tuesday night I received a tear-filled e-mail from her saying that she wanted to accept God in her life. I was elated and then she told me that another friend of hers had called her and said, "I love you, but you are on a path to destruction and you're going to hell!" That phone call changed her life. I told her then, "If that's all I had to say, I would have said that years ago!" But you just never know when all that has been planted and watered will result in God's increase.

Before Apostle Skinner died, he may have never seen this young man again, but only God knows if he will meet him again in heaven—all because he laid a foundation of truth in God. Don't deny who you are in Christ—continue to lay the groundwork in the hearts and lives of the people you come in contact with, and God will do the rest.

*Acting is all about honesty. If you can fake that, you've got it made.*

—George Burns

## HAMMING IT UP!

In many of our churches the emphasis is not necessarily on the content, theology or exhortation of the message. Unfortunately messages are judged by the delivery, presentation, humor and even the appearance of the speaker. Oftentimes the message delivered in some churches is almost incoherent. Such was the case of one minister I know of who informed me that he would just throw in a word during the pauses of his preaching to see the reaction of the congregation.

As in a lot of these messages, very few Bible passages were utilized. In fact, only one was given. It was in the beginning of the message and never related to again. The preacher built to a slow boil and then began to really get down. In between each pause he'd yell out "HAM!" and the people would respond enthusiastically more and more. Before you knew it, they'd be shouting and praising God each and every time he said, "Ham!" Can you believe members of a church were shouting off the word "ham"? Unbelievable!

**Reverend Patricia S. Webster** is the senior pastor of Shiloh Pentecostal Church, Inc.–Christian Love Center in Somerville, New Jersey, and is also the mother of the author.

The Bible says: *He that hath an ear, let him hear what the Spirit saith unto the churches.* (Revelation 2:7)

## Reflection

There are so many scriptural references about hearing. From David asking the Lord to "hear his prayer, O God; give ear to the words of my mouth" (Psalm 54:2) to John the Revelator admonishing those who have an ear to hear, we should listen to what the Spirit is saying to the churches. Hearing and listening are two key words that are essential to the body of Christ. We must incline our ear to hear God and we must listen for His voice and clear direction. Those who were shouting off of the word "ham" were unfortunately not listening, but getting caught up in the emotion that can sometimes come with the preached word. We must be like the Bereans who listened intently and then went home and studied the scripture for themselves. By doing so, you'll be less prone to jump out of your seat when a ham is in the pulpit.

# *Laugh Stop*

### *Pray for Me*

One Sunday in a Midwest city, a young child was "acting up" during the morning worship hour. The parents did their best to maintain some sense of order in the pew but were losing the battle. Finally, the father picked the little fellow up and walked sternly up the aisle on his way out. Just before reaching the safety of the foyer, the little one called loudly to the congregation, "Pray for me! Pray for me!"

### *Make Me Better, Lord*

A little boy was overheard praying: "Lord, if you can't make me a better boy, don't worry about it. I'm having a real good time like I am."

### *Thrown Out of Heaven*

A father was at the beach with his children when the four-year-old son ran up to him, grabbed his hand and led him to the shore, where a seagull lay dead in the sand. "Daddy, what happened to him?" the son asked. "He died and went to Heaven," the dad replied. The boy thought a moment and then said, "Did God throw him back down?"

### Poor Preacher

After the church service a little boy told the pastor, "When I grow up, I'm going to give you some money." "Well, thank you," the pastor replied. "But why?" "Because my daddy says you're one of the poorest preachers we've ever had."

*Most human beings have an infinite capacity for tak-*
*ing things for granted.*

—Aldous Huxley

## TONGUE-TIED

A homeless man came to our church this one Sunday morning. After some time he began making his way down the aisle. The pastor assumed he wanted to be saved! So he told the church, "Saints, this man wants to give his life to God!" The church members erupted in praise as the deacons started to "help" him down the aisle. They were so busy shouting that they didn't hear him saying, "MMMMM." The homeless man got louder: "MMMMMM." The deacons heard him and said, "He's speaking in tongues!" The congregation really started to shout at this time. The homeless man continued, "MMM-MMM!" As he got to the altar, they all quieted down so that they could hear him speak, and to their astonishment he blurted out, "MY PANTS ARE FALLING DOWN!"

**Mary Mary** is a successful gospel duo, consisting of sisters Erica Monique Campbell and Trecina "Tina" Evette Campbell, and they are often credited for broadening the fan base of urban contemporary gospel by introducing elements of rhythm and blues and hip-hop into their performances and songwriting. Besides being behind the scenes of numerous artists and projects, they are also known for hits such as "Yesterday" and "Shackles (Praise You)."

The Bible says: *I thank God that I speak in tongues more than all of you. But in the church I would rather speak five intelligible words to instruct others than ten thousand words in a tongue.* (1 Corinthians 14:18–19, NIV)

## Reflection

In our exuberance in winning the lost, we often forget that they are still people. In Christian history the missionaries' zeal to win the "barbarians" was such that we forgot to actually show them respect and the love of Christ. Many times it was in fact an attempt to Westernize rather than to Christianize. We all have problems properly articulating ourselves from time to time. Though this happens, we must remember that we all still have a voice. No matter how mumbled it may be.

*The winds of the Spirit are always blowing. Some people put up windbreaks and others open up their windows.*

—Author Unknown

## SHE RODE A HONDA

In the early days of Pentecostalism in the United States within the large and not so large denominations, the baptism of the Holy Spirit, with what they termed the evidence of speaking in other tongues, was very much stressed. Today there isn't nearly the emphasis on this practice as was in the early to mid-1990s.

However, every now and then a revival will break out and this gift is attempted to be induced on those who have never partaken. On one such Friday night revival those who had not spoken in tongues were prodded to come up to receive this special anointing. One young gentleman came up politely, but reluctantly. The elder who was assigned to this young man began to pray with him and command that he speak this heavenly language. Nothing happened.

Eventually through a bit of peer pressure and exhaustion, he began to stammer, "She rode a Honda. She rode a Honda," hoping that this would fool the elder and allow him to return to his seat. The elder, a very conservative and old-time saint of God, could not contain himself and burst out laughing right up there in the pulpit area and allowed the young man to return to his seat.

**Randy Vaughan** is an author and member of Shiloh Pentecostal Church, Inc.–Christian Love Center in Somerville, New Jersey.

> The Bible says: *So I say to you, ask, and it will be given to you; seek, and you will find; knock, and it will be opened to you. For everyone who asks receives, and he who seeks finds, and to him who knocks it will be opened. If a son asks for bread from any father among you, will he give him a stone? Or if he asks for a fish, will he give him a serpent instead of a fish? Or if he asks for an egg, will he offer him a scorpion? If you then, being evil, know how to give good gifts to your children, how much more will your heavenly Father give the Holy Spirit to those who ask Him!"* (Luke 11:9–13, NIV)

## Reflection

The more advanced we become in our research and understanding of God, the more we are led to the inevitable conclusion that He's still a mystery.

*An honest man's the noblest work of God.*

—Alexander Pope

## SLAIN IN THE SPIRIT, OR NOT?

At a church we attended previously, there was one particular member who, without fail, would catch the Holy Ghost at pretty much the same time every Sunday. On this particular Sunday, she raised her level of performance and started the proverbial "flipping over pews, foaming at the mouth and falling on the floor". . . the usual ritual. Now, my husband had been suspicious of the sincerity of her divine experiences after seeing it occur consistently every Sunday at nearly the same time. On this day, his suspicions were confirmed. Being immune to the experience, I was not paying her any attention and was focusing on the services. Due to the extended duration of her lying prostrate on the floor in the aisle, my husband decided to continue to watch the show and noticed something quite comical: she peeked to see if anyone was watching or coming to help (picture someone strewn on the floor peeking up). He could not stop laughing. After she saw no one was coming her way, she promptly got up, straightened her clothes and went back to her seat. As quickly as the Holy Ghost came, it went.

**Kenneth A. Myles** is a native of Saginaw, Michigan, and is employed by Procter & Gamble in Cincinnati, Ohio. He serves as a board member for Greater Cincinnati Behavioral Health Services and is president and CEO of KAMJAM Entertainment. **Sonia J. Myles,** also a native of Saginaw, Michigan, is director of Global Media Purchases for Procter & Gamble and serves as a board member for Impact Young Lives, Women Helping Women, and as advisory board chair for Florida A&M University's School of Business and Industry (her alma mater). They are the proud parents of Kendall, twelve, and Jordan, ten. Sonia is currently completing her first book, entitled *7 Spirit-Filled Strategies for Raising a Loving Child.*

The Bible says: *The wisdom of the prudent [is] to understand his way: but the folly of fools [is] deceit.* (Proverbs 14:8)

## Reflection

Deceit is a dishonest act or statement. Deception is the act of deceiving someone—until you get caught. How easy is it to say that you are a follower of Christ but you really aren't? How easy is it to say you love or like someone, but you really can't stand the person? How easy is it to tell someone else how he or she should live but your life is in a shambles? Most of us can be guilty of deceit at least one time in our lives. But whom are we fooling? People. Probably. God. Absolutely not! God sees and knows everything and you can never deceive Him, no matter where you hide, where you run or how hard you try. Good works and acts of worship may convince the world we are faithful to God. But the Lord knows our intentions. Only through honoring Him with our daily obedience can we unlock His heart. There's a quote: "Hide nothing, for time, which sees all and hears all, exposes all." I'm going to change that to say: "Hide nothing, for GOD, who sees all, hears all, knows and created all, exposes all"—even when you are peeking from the floor.

# Humor in the Bible

## A LITTLE TEASING NEVER HURT ANYONE

Periodically in the Old Testament when individuals are referred to as "prophesying," it typically meant what we today refer to as "speaking in tongues." In the following passage we have one of the very few times in the Bible where someone is making explicit statements intended to generate laughs.

Elijah, in an attempt to prove the authenticity of his God, challenges the Baal prophets to a duel. Whichever God shows up to devour and burn wood would be the real God.

The Bible says: *Then Elijah said to them, "I am the only one of the Lord's prophets left, but Baal has four hundred and fifty prophets. Get two bulls for us. Let them choose one for themselves, and let them cut it into pieces and put it on the wood but not set fire to it. I will prepare the other bull and put it on the wood but not set fire to it. Then you call on the name of your god, and I will call on the name of the LORD. The god who answers by fire—he is God."* *Then all the people said, "What you say is good." Elijah said to the prophets of Baal, "Choose one of the bulls and*

*prepare it first, since there are so many of you. Call on
the name of your god, but do not light the fire." So they
took the bull given them and prepared it. Then they called
on the name of Baal from morning till noon. "O Baal, answer us!" they shouted. But there was no response; no one
answered. And they danced around the altar they had made.
At noon Elijah began to taunt them. "Shout louder!" he said.
"Surely he is a god! Perhaps he is deep in thought, or busy,
or traveling. Maybe he is sleeping and must be awakened."
So they shouted louder and slashed themselves with swords
and spears, as was their custom, until their blood flowed.
Midday passed, and they continued their frantic prophesying
until the time for the evening sacrifice. But there was no
response, no one answered, no one paid attention.* (1 Kings
18:22–38, NIV)

Now, this kind of taunting isn't recommended, especially toward fanatics who don't mind cutting themselves with knives.
However, if you can imagine, it must've been pretty challenging
for those individuals who happened to be standing around watching this spectacle to contain themselves from laughing heartily.

Who could blame Elijah? These false prophets would not
stop with their antics and fanaticism. Eventually they probably just prophesied themselves to exhaustion.

After waiting for several hours, Elijah simply could not handle the boredom any longer and began to do a little teasing.
"Shout louder!" and "Surely he is a god! Perhaps he is deep in
thought, or busy, or traveling," Elijah exclaimed. Seeing their
little god on a train with a suitcase is quite funny.

Interestingly, as brazen as Elijah is with the prophets of Baal, he is equally cowardly when it comes to Jezebel the queen. When she catches wind of his actions, all fury is let loose and he decides to hide. Hell has no fury like a woman . . . scorned. The fact of the matter is that many of the prophets during the Old Testament times were afraid. Many had been killed. Even though miracles were worked through Elijah, they were no guarantee against Jezebel. Eventually Jezebel would meet her violent end, which must have drawn a hearty "whew" from Elijah.

Hmmm . . . not afraid of hundreds of masochistic fanatics, but a crazed woman causes him to hide in the mountains?

## GETTING INTO THE ACT

Here we have King Saul. This is after he is named king. After David has defeated Goliath. Unfortunately the relationship between Saul and David has turned sour. Saul, being king, had the upper hand and was trying to have David murdered. David went on the lam. He hid out for quite a while from Saul. Finally Saul had a GPS on David and sent out his henchmen to take care of him at Naioth in Ramah.

Each time the soldiers went to apprehend David, they ran into the prophet Samuel and had an unusual encounter with the Spirit of God and they began to prophesy.

Prophesying should be explained as not being the foretelling of the future or even *just* speaking for the Lord. In some passages of the Bible it can be interpreted this way. However, in this and a few other passages it means glossalia or, as we say today, "speaking in tongues."

> The Bible says: *Now it was told Saul, saying, "Take note, David is at Naioth in Ramah!" Then Saul sent messengers to take David. And when they saw the group of prophets prophesying, and Samuel standing as leader over them, the Spirit of God came upon the messengers of Saul, and they also prophesied. And when Saul was told, he sent other messengers, and they prophesied likewise. Then Saul sent messengers again the third time, and they prophesied also. Then he also went to Ramah, and came to the great well that is at Sechu. So he asked, and said, "Where are Samuel and David?" And someone said, "Indeed they are at Naioth in Ramah." So he went there to Naioth in Ramah. Then the Spirit of God was upon him also, and he went on and prophesied until he came to Naioth in Ramah.* (1 Samuel 19–23, NIV)

Three times Saul sent messengers to David and Samuel, and each time they encountered some Pentecostals and succumbed to the Spirit of God. Eventually even Saul, the king himself, could not be contained and went to see what the problem was and ended up joining this local group of Pentecostals as well.

Well, if you can't beat 'em . . . then pray with 'em.

# CHAPTER FIVE

## Love Never Fails

~

*Love feels no burden, thinks nothing of trouble,*
*attempts what is above its strength. . . .*
*It is therefore able to undertake all things, and*
*it completes many things, and warrants them to*
*take effect, where he who does not love would*
*faint and lie down.*

—Thomas à Kempis

How many of us have gone into a church and heard great preaching and an awesome choir? In fact, it seemed as if the whole church had its stuff really together. Yet were left with that feeling of emptiness—the feeling that no one even noticed that we were there. It's the same feeling we get when someone gives us something out of compulsion. We'd rather have a modest gift given with true love.

The Apostle Paul says we can have the gifts, but lack love and those gifts wouldn't matter. This is hard for us to understand today. We live in a world where money and power mean everything.

The Bible says: *If I speak in the tongues of men and of angels, but have not love, I am only a resounding gong or a clanging cymbal. If I have the gift of prophecy and can fathom all mysteries and all knowledge, and if I have a faith that can move mountains, but have not love, I am nothing. If I give all I possess to the poor and surrender my body to the flames, but have not love, I gain nothing.* (1 Corinthians 13:1–3, NIV)

Jesus asked the question whether it was easier to get healed or to forgive sins. The obvious answer to the rhetorical question was that it was easier to have sins forgiven. Even for the savior himself. Jesus did not always heal everyone He came in contact with. Most of us either don't know how to receive healing or simply don't know God's will. Yet we will gladly take the love that will set us free. The love that will guarantee us eternal life. The love that forgives.

The unconditional love of a mother and father. The unconditional love of a brother and/or sister. The unconditional love of a spouse or a friend. This is the kind of love that can make a man on his deathbed feel no pain. It's this kind of love that can make a mother's kiss on a little boy's boo-boo on his finger feel much better. No, it doesn't take away the actual rigors of life. It just makes them more manageable. Love never fails.

*Earth laughs in flowers.*

—Ralph Waldo Emerson

## LIGHTS OUT!

I'm a preacher who uses illustrations often to get God's message across. It's a great way to demonstrate what God is trying to say to His people in a visual way. On this particular Sunday morning at World Changers Church International (WCCI) in Atlanta, Georgia, I was led to use an illustration—but had no idea using this illustration would turn into such mayhem.

So it was Sunday morning, and all was well at WCCI. Praise and worship had gone forth. The choir had sung. Offering had been given. Now it was time for the Word. In order to demonstrate what God wanted people to hear, I engaged the help of one of my executive assistants. Cornelius came to the podium in place of me and started to read my resignation letter. In the letter, I informed the church that I was resigning from being the pastor of WCCI. I told the church I had had it and I would no longer be preaching the Gospel every Sunday morning. The administrator then asked that the church lights be turned off— as this would be the last day for the doors of World Changers Church International to be open.

As I stood in the background, all of a sudden mayhem broke loose. People started crying and screaming, "NO, PASTOR,

NO!" Not expecting this turn of events, I immediately told my assistant to have the lights turned on. When the lights came up, I stepped forth, prepared to tell the church that I was just illustrating the message God was to have me preach. However, my assistant turned to the left and laughter overcame him. Why? I could not believe my eyes. My head of security, a big, burly man, was tucked in the corner of the church crying like a little baby! It was then I could not contain my laughter. Of all the sights I never thought I would behold, that was surely one of them!

**Dr. Creflo A. Dollar** is the senior pastor of World Changers Church International with churches in College Park, Georgia; New York City; and Battle Creek, Michigan. His daily broadcast, *Changing Your World*, can be seen in most countries around the world.

The Bible says: *And let us not be weary in well doing: for in due season we shall reap, if we faint not.* (Galatians 6:9)

## Reflection

Pastors are special people. I truly believe you have to have a unique anointing from God to be called to Pastor. But although the illustration took an unexpected turn, the relevancy of what God was trying to say was clear. How do you think He feels when we quit on Him? It's so often in the body of Christ that one infraction will cause someone to say, "I quit!" Someone looks at you the wrong way: "I quit!" Another member may not speak to you in church: "I quit!" You don't get your way in the church meeting: "I quit!" But look at God! "The spirit of God has made me and breath of the Almighty has given me life" (Job 33:4)—He's the reason we move and breathe and feel and taste and touch and smell and live. But He NEVER quits on us. When we turn our back on Him, when we go another way, God never leaves us or forsakes us. Why? Because He loves us. So next time you are thinking about giving up, remember, God has never quit on you—don't quit on Him.

*For neither man nor angel can discern Hypocrisy, the only evil that walks invisible, except to God alone.*

—John Milton, *Paradise Lost*

## THE MISSION FIELD

Billy Graham is alleged to have said, "The greatest mission field is on the church rolls."

**William Franklin Graham, Jr.** (better known as Billy Graham) is an evangelist and a spiritual adviser to multiple U.S. presidents. He is a member of the Southern Baptist Convention. Graham has preached in person to more people around the world than anyone who has ever lived. As of 1993, more than 2.5 million people had stepped forward at his crusades to "accept Jesus Christ as their personal savior." As of 2002, Graham's lifetime audience, including radio and television broadcasts, topped 2 billion. He is also the author of multiple best-selling books.

The Bible says: *Then he said to his disciples, "The harvest is plentiful but the workers are few. Ask the Lord of the harvest, therefore, to send out workers into his harvest field."* (Matthew 9:27–28, NIV)

## Reflection

Those who live outside of the church tend to point out the hypocrisy of Christians more than any other shortcoming. Their mistake has been to assume that all of those who attend church are in fact Christians. Subsequently they label them hypocrites, but it would be better stated if we said they were simple sinners. Even for those who are hypocrites, one cannot argue that they are in the best place to change.

*You reach a point where you don't work for money.*

—Walt Disney

## BY ANY MEANS NECESSARY

There was an older woman who was over the children's choir and the children were always acting up in rehearsal. So one night at rehearsal the woman was fed up with the kids' bad behavior. Needing a break, she went downstairs to use the restroom and came back upstairs to see the children were still misbehaving. That was it. She lost her composure and began to yell at them to behave and told them that they would act right and sing the songs properly because she would not have them embarrass her in front of the whole church on Sunday. All the children were quiet and just staring at her. She was thinking, "Wow, I guess they are ready to listen now," and she looked down at herself only to see that her T-shirt bearing the church's name was pulled up over her bra and that her chest had been exposed to all the children the entire time she had been yelling. She never felt a breeze because her jean skirt was tucked just underneath her bra. Needless to say, the children had a story to tell all their parents when they got home from rehearsal.

**Johnnie "Smurf" Smith** is a Grammy-nominated producer from New Jerusalem Temple of the Living God in Camden, New Jersey.

The Bible says: *They are spirits of demons performing miraculous signs, and they go out to the kings of the whole world,
to gather them for the battle on the great day of God Almighty.
"Behold, I come like a thief! Blessed is he who stays awake
and keeps his clothes with him, so that he may not go naked
and be shamefully exposed."* (Revelation 16:14–16, NIV)

## Reflection

Malcolm X's most famous phrase was probably, "By any
means necessary." The previous story reflects the age-old frustration commonly shared by any adult who has worked with
children in church. It's the youths who are bored against the
adult who's attempting to get the best out of them. The adult
can claim the victory when they become adults and must face
the same frustrations. In the meantime it's . . . by any means
necessary to keep them in church and involved. During that
time desperation often causes us to reveal our innermost self.
Sometimes it even causes us to . . . expose too much of ourselves.

# *Laugh Stop*

### Whom Can You Trust?

Little Rodney, four years old, walked down the beach, and as he did, he spied a woman sitting under a beach umbrella on the sand. He walked up to her and asked, "Are you a Christian?" "Yes," she replied. "Do you read your Bible every day?" She nodded her head and said, "Yes." "Do you pray often?" the boy asked next, and again she answered, "Yes." With that he asked his final question, "Will you hold my quarter while I go swimming?"

### Prayer of Patience

Timmy had been misbehaving and was sent to his room. After a while he emerged and informed his mother that he had thought it over and then said a prayer. "Fine," said the pleased mother. "If you ask God to help you not misbehave, He will help you." "Oh, I didn't ask Him to help me not misbehave," said Timmy. "I asked Him to help you put up with me."

### The Money Bowl

A small boy stunned his parents when he began to empty his pockets of nickels, dimes and quarters. Finally his mother said, "Where did you get all that money?" "At Sunday School," the boy replied nonchalantly. "They have bowls of it."

*An optimist laughs to forget, a pessimist forgets to laugh.*

—Anonymous

## THE SWORD OF THE LORD

A good ole tent revival. Do you remember those days when you were young and every summer you had a tent revival where you were hot and sweaty but free to worship? Truly uninhibited praise. In the context of this book, we're going to say that this particular tent service that I went to was a church—because it was utilized for us as well during that week.

I can't remember if it was during the week or the weekend, but we were having our annual tent revival. My church was in New York, and those who would come to the tent revival would be from all walks of life—drug dealers, prostitutes, those who felt they were down on their luck and those who had a street survival mentality. Well, this particular service we were having testimonies, and a woman, who just got saved, stood up to share how the Lord had spared her life. Here's her story:

"I was walking down the street on my way to the tent revival when a robber came up and asked me to give him my money. I told him no because I was standing on the sword of the Lord. He asked me again, so I reached down in my bosom and pulled out my sword and I began to smite him."

My pastor immediately jumped up and said, "What are you saying?" She proceeded to tell him that she had done the Lord's service. He said, "No, sis, you committed a felony!"

**Jeff Robinson** is the CEO of MBK Entertainment in New York.

The Bible says: *"Dearly beloved, avenge not yourselves, but [rather] give place unto wrath: for it is written, Vengeance [is] mine; I will repay, saith the Lord."* (Romans 12:19)

## Reflection

Although Christians universally and overwhelmingly agree that the Bible is God's Word, there are those times when they can be just as overwhelmingly disagreeable about certain parts of the Bible. One example is the commandment to turn the other cheek. Most Christians typically smirk when this is brought up with a "yeah right" kind of response. The initial response would be to retaliate. But when we realize that God will handle EVERY situation, we are able to understand that we don't have to worry about a thing. Don't commit a felony in the name of the Lord—let God work it out for you.

*It's easier to find a new audience than to write a new speech.*

—Dan Kennedy

## JACK BENNY VERSUS BILLY GRAHAM

Jack Benny states, in commenting about a meeting with Billy Graham, "One of the Reverend Graham's wittiest lines came when I remarked that once when I was drawing great crowds to my comedy shows at the London Palladium he had been drawing about five hundred thousand people in one week to his meetings in London. This was true. We had both been in London at the same time in 1954. Humbly he said he couldn't take the credit for his success: 'Look at the writers I have, Jack.' 'Writers?' I questioned. The Reverend Graham continued, 'Yes . . . Isaiah . . . Jeremiah . . . Matthew, Mark, Luke and John.' "

**William Franklin Graham, Jr.** (better known as Billy Graham) is an evangelist and a spiritual adviser to multiple U.S. presidents. He is a member of the Southern Baptist Convention. Graham has preached in person to more people around the world than anyone who has ever lived. As of 1993, more than 2.5 million people had stepped forward at his crusades to "accept Jesus Christ as their personal savior." As of 2002, Graham's lifetime audience, including radio and television broadcasts, topped 2 billion. He is also the author of multiple best-selling books.

The Bible says: *Now the temple was crowded with men and women; all the rulers of the Philistines were there, and on the roof were about three thousand men and women watching Samson perform.* (Judges 16:27, NIV)

## Reflection

The great comedy team of Abbott and Costello was known for doing hilarious skits. Most notable was the "Who's On First?" bit. What most people today don't realize is that many of these comedic routines are old vaudevillian sketches. Abbott and Costello removed the vulgarity to appeal to a wider audience as well as get the timing down perfectly.

This is similar to what takes place when the Gospel is preached. It's a two-thousand-year-old routine that not only seems to get better, but continues to attract larger crowds.

*Laughter is like medicine to the soul.*

—Author Unknown

## THE PURSE THIEF

A young prophet was preaching at a church when a woman came up and told him she needed healing for a bad back. The prophet prayed over the woman and told her, "I hear the Lord telling me to have you run until your healing is manifested." So the woman put her purse on her shoulder and started to run around the church. After the first time, the prophet asked her how she was feeling. She said, "I'm doing okay . . . but not feeling that great." So the prophet told her to run again. She ran around again. Again, she didn't feel 100 percent. So he said to run again. This time when she ran, her purse fell off. She came back to the prophet, and he said, "The Lord says run, run, run." So she started running only to see that her purse was no longer where she'd dropped it. She came to the front and tried to tell the prophet that her purse was gone—he ignored her and told her to run on. She ran around again. She came back to try to say AGAIN that her purse was gone. He said, "I'm telling you, this should be the last time, RUN, I say, RUN!" She ran around and he asked her, "How are you feeling?" She looked at him, took the microphone and clearly said, "I'm feeling fine but my

God * !@* purse is GONE!" Suffice it to say, the prophet immediately covered up the microphone.

**Charles Brown** is the musical director and a member of Shiloh Pentecostal Church, Inc.-Christian Love Center in Somerville, New Jersey.

> The Bible says: *So I said: "Woe is me, for I am undone! Because I am a man of unclean lips, And I dwell in the midst of a people of unclean lips; For my eyes have seen the King, The LORD of hosts." Then one of the seraphim flew to me, having in his hand a live coal which he had taken with the tongs from the altar. And he touched my mouth with it, and said: "Behold, this has touched your lips; Your iniquity is taken away, And your sin purged."* (Isaiah 6:5–7)

> *. . . for out of the abundance of the heart, the mouth spiked!* (Matthew 12:34)

## Reflection

How often does something slip out of our mouths that we do not want or expect to say? The Bible teaches us that "out of the abundance of the heart, the mouth speaks," and because of that, whatever you really feel or think becomes a part of your heart. So in order to say only the words that God will have you speak—words of love, encouragement, peace and hope—it is necessary for each of us to do as Paul suggests in Philippians 4:8: "Finally, brethren, whatsoever things are true, whatsoever things [are] honest, whatsoever things [are] just, whatsoever things [are] pure, whatsoever things [are] lovely, whatsoever things [are] of good report; if [there be] any virtue, and if [there be] any praise, think on these things." When we keep our thoughts heavenly and Godly and we meditate on the goodness of God, our hearts will be pure and then our mouths will speak only good things.

# *Laugh Stop*

### Where Is God?

A couple had two little boys, ages eight and ten, who were excessively mischievous. The two were always getting into trouble and their parents could be assured that if any mischief occurred in their town their two young sons were in some way involved. The parents were at their wit's end as to what to do about their sons' behavior. The mother had heard that a clergyman in town had been successful in disciplining children in the past, so she asked her husband if he thought they should send the boys to speak with the clergyman. The husband said, "We might as well. We need to do something before I really lose my temper!" The clergyman agreed to speak with the boys, but asked to see them individually. The eight-year-old went to meet with him first. The clergyman sat the boy down and asked him sternly, "Where is God?" The boy made no response, so the clergyman repeated the question in an even sterner tone, "Where is God?!" Again the boy made no attempt to answer. So the clergyman raised his voice even more and shook his finger in the boy's face. "WHERE IS GOD?!" At that, the boy bolted from the room and ran directly home, slamming himself in a closet. His older brother followed him into the closet and asked what had happened. The younger brother replied, "We are in BIG trouble this time. God is missing and they think we did it!"

### Shhhhhh . . .

A Sunday School teacher asked the children just before she dismissed them to go back to the church, "And why is it necessary to be quiet in church?" One little boy jumped up and yelled, "Because people are sleeping!"

❧

*Always do sober what you said you'd do drunk. That will teach you to keep your mouth shut.*

—Ernest Hemingway

## TUESDAY NIGHT BUBBLE STUDY

Being part of a start-up church is not easy. Finding a place to worship and increasing attendance are just a sampling of the hurdles that are faced. In those days we worshipped at a local youth club. As far as other events we had to meet at various members' homes, as the leaders did not live within that area.

On one such Tuesday Night Bible Study we went to Sister Betty's house. Sister Betty was a dear, sweet woman of the Lord who loved to volunteer for several of the assignments in our fledgling church. She was always punctual and timely, so it came as a shock when we were all standing outside her home knocking for about fifteen minutes. One of those standing with us was one of her best friends. She assured us that Betty was definitely inside. We waited and waited.

Eventually the door squeaked open slowly and around peered one of her eyes. She smiled broadly and let us all into her home, which was simmering with the smell of alcohol. We attempted to just ignore her as she repeated everything being said. "Tun ta Fust Cuhinthians . . . chattuh fuhteen." Eventually we just gave in and decided to have prayer for her instead.

Author unknown.

The Bible says: *But Jesus bent down and started to write on the ground with his finger. When they kept on questioning him, he straightened up and said to them, "If any one of you is without sin, let him be the first to throw a stone at her."* (John 8:7, NIV)

## Reflection

To a certain degree we can be admirers of politicians, especially those who run our government on a higher level and in very visible positions such as governors, senators and the president. While there will be some who will critically ask, "why?" it's actually for that reason. They take a heap of criticism that most of the population could not endure. Their lives are examined under a microscope from the time of their childhood until today. Nothing is left unturned as every acquaintance and video clip is rewound to examine every word and deed. Who can really live under such scrutiny? This is what we should remember when judging another.

*A rich man may be wise in his own eyes, but a poor man who has discernment sees through him.*

—King Solomon

## SIX IN A SEAT

I grew up in church, Church of God in Christ, to be exact. If you were raised COGIC (that's what we call it), you know that you can see some pretty heavy stuff like this story!

It was a Friday night and we were having a church revival. My mom, my sisters and I were at church, as was normal with us kids. Now, I want you to keep this thought in the back of you mind: my mom was KNOWN for always offering to drive someone home. She was the "Notorious Driver." Anywho. As we were in church praising the Lord, what appeared to be a corporate-looking woman in a business suit came in. The kids were sitting in the back of the church, and as the woman started walking down the aisle, all of a sudden one of the church mothers jumped up, and started stomping her foot and yelling at the top of her lungs, "JESUS!" We didn't know what the heck was going on. Next thing we knew, strong women of God surrounded the woman. They wrapped her in a sheet, and she looked as though she had turned into a serpent—writhing, long venomous tongue and everything! Scared does not begin to describe what we were feeling. But through calling on the name of Jesus, the demon departed and the woman returned to her normal self.

So, now church is over and the woman was sitting at the front of the church and asked, "Anybody going to Queens?" Why the heck did my mother say, "Sure, come with us"? I was, like, you are not letting that demon in the car with us. But here we go—all seven of us to Queens, New York. Well, there was no way I was letting those kids in the backseat with a demonized woman. So I made all four kids plus my mother and I sit in the front seat of the car. The poor woman kept inviting the kids to the back, but I assured her, "We ride like this all the time." If anybody saw us on Queens Boulevard, I'm sure they got a good laugh or thought we were crazy. But I must say, the woman was changed forever, sitting in the back, talking as normal as I was—never realizing the deliverance that God had given her that day. It allowed me to see God's transforming power right before my eyes. But I still didn't get into the backseat with her.

**Tichina Arnold** is an award-winning actress best known for her role as Pam on *Martin*. She currently plays the lead role on *Everybody Hates Chris,* the highly successful television series based on the life of comedian Chris Rock.

The Bible says: *The demons begged Jesus, "If you drive us out, send us into the herd of pigs." He said to them, "Go!" So they came out and went into the pigs, and the whole herd rushed down the steep bank into the lake and died in the water. Those tending the pigs ran off, went into the town and reported all this, including what had happened to the demon-possessed men.* (Matthew 8:31–33, NIV)

## Reflection

Don't you want to be so in tune to God that you can immediately spot a demon? Jesus could. The Bible gives numerous examples of Jesus calling out demons and restoring men and women to their right mind. Satanic power is real—don't be fooled. If anyone tells you Satan doesn't exist—he or she is a liar! And his demonic forces are evident in today's world—through people, through circumstances, through situations. As funny as this story is, it's a real truth that there are people today who still have to be exorcised. *The Exorcist* is probably one of the most vivid theatrical examples of demonic power. But do we have to fear? NO WAY! Even the demons tremble at the name of Jesus Christ! The scripture in Matthew 8:31–33 proves that. Demons recognize God's power and authority. So, "if God be for us, WHO shall be against us?" No demon in hell; just don't give him a ride home!

*Laughter is an instant vacation.*

—Milton Berle

## MAY WE ALL STAND?

An elderly pastor took his seat in a side "boothlike" extension of the pulpit. This is something many churches still practice as a way of recognizing those who have served in ministry as a pastor, but are no longer active. Typically they are designated "pastor emeritus."

He had requested access to a live microphone during each service. His age prevented him from standing or preaching. This specially designated area and microphone setup allowed him to have some participation and visibility as the head pastor of the church. During the service, suddenly the elderly pastor's voice was heard, deeply and slowly, as he said, "May we all stand," and everyone obeyed and stood to his or her feet. Nothing else was said, so the congregants politely sat back in their seats. Moments later the command resounded, "May we all stand," and like skeptical robots, the congregants stood to their feet. Again, nothing further was spoken. After another incident of interrupting confusion, it became apparent that the pastor could no longer have access to a live microphone.

**Sheila Jones** is an anointed woman of God and oversees the Drama Ministry, among other things, at Shiloh Pentecostal Church, Inc.–Christian Love Center in Somerville, New Jersey.

> The Bible says: *The watchman opens the gate for him, and the sheep listen to his voice. He calls his own sheep by name and leads them out. When he has brought out all his own, he goes on ahead of them, and his sheep follow him because they know his voice. But they will never follow a stranger; in fact, they will run away from him because they do not recognize a stranger's voice.* (John 10:3–5, NIV)

## Reflection

In the childhood game of Simon Says, we are told to do things only when Simon says to do them. If that phrase, "Simon Says," is not used, we are to ignore the command. This fights against our natural instinct, which is simply to follow orders no matter where they come from. You can literally walk up to a stranger and say, "Don't sit here, sit there," and without hesitation, most people will just comply.

People tend to question the instructions of those who have the most concern and the most expertise. Typically their advice lacks what we wanted to hear or it comes at a time when we don't want to receive it. It's that rebellious youth inside of us all that tells us to "question authority." Wouldn't our lives be a lot better if we could just learn to only listen to and obey the true Voice of Authority?

# ℋumor in the ℬible

## Who's Fooling Whom?

Apparently there is a little teasing in the personality of Samson. Most of us are already informed in regards to Delilah's contribution to Samson's downfall. Many are possibly not aware as to what she went through to get him to the point of deception.

She, after being paid quite a hefty amount by Philistine representatives in retaliation for the havoc he put their society through, was induced to set him up and find out how he got and could lose his strength. When he would lose his strength was when they would apprehend him and exact retribution.

So Delilah said to Samson, "Tell me the secret of your great strength and how you can be tied up and subdued." Samson answered her, "If anyone ties me with seven fresh thongs that have not been dried, I'll become as weak as any other man." Then the rulers of the Philistines brought her seven fresh thongs that had not been dried, and she tied him with them. With men hidden in the room, she called to him, "Samson, the Philistines are upon you!" But he snapped the thongs as easily as a piece of string snaps when it comes close to a flame. So the secret of his strength was not discovered. Then Delilah said to Samson, "You have made a fool of me; you lied to me. Come now, tell me how you can be tied." He said, "If anyone ties me securely with new ropes that have never been used, I'll become as weak as any other man." So Delilah took new ropes and tied him with them.

Then, with men hidden in the room, she called to him, "Samson, the Philistines are upon you!" But he snapped the ropes off his arms as if they were threads. Delilah then said to Samson, "Until now, you have been making a fool of me and lying to me. Tell me how you can be tied." He replied, "If you weave the seven braids of my head into the fabric on the loom and tighten it with the pin, I'll become as weak as any other man." So while he was sleeping, Delilah took the seven braids of his head, wove them into the fabric and tightened it with the pin. Again she called to him, "Samson, the Philistines are upon you!" He awoke from his sleep and pulled up the pin and the loom, with the fabric. Then she said to him, "How can you say, 'I love you,' when you won't confide in me? This is the third time you have made a fool of me and haven't told me the secret of your great strength." With such nagging she prodded him day after day until he was tired to death.

This particular section of Samson's escapades has two humorous parts. The first part is how Samson continually told lies to Delilah in regards to how to weaken him. He goes from tying him with seven fresh thongs (not today's version), then goes, "No, no, no, that's not it." Then he goes, "I'll tell you what. It's new ropes. Yeah, that's it . . . new ropes. Tie me up with new ropes and there you go." Of course, Samson must apologize again and then really tell the truth this time. His last laugh is having his braided hair intertwined with fabric. "Fooled you again!" he must have exclaimed. In Judges 16:10, Delilah says, "You have made a fool of me!" (Talk about the pot calling the kettle black!)

The second part of this laugher is right at the end. The writer infers that *"she nagged him to death!"* Rarely is symbolic language so explicitly used in the Old or New Testament. It seems to resemble our twenty-first-century language. The writer seems to have had personal experience with being nagged to death.

With such nagging she prodded him day after day until he was tired to death.

There's probably a bunch of men out there right now going, "Yep, I understand."

Of course, the story is tragic as Samson does reveal the source of his strength. What most people fail to notice is that the haircutting itself is not done by Delilah, but one of her servants. Talk about not wanting to get your hands dirty.

His demise is heart wrenching as he is blinded and made to do the work of oxen and eventually made sport of for spectators. His revenge is complete when he is able to bring down a stadium full of his tormentors.

He who laughs last laughs loudest.


## Are You Crazy, Paul?

Paul is not always on the giving end of sarcasm. He has been on the receiving end of it as well. Paul, who has fourteen New Testament documents attributed to him, was not so unlike modern-day Christians in that he was also called a fanatic, crazy and probably out of his mind occasionally.

Paul, by his own admission, was educated formally at a high level. Acts attributes his learning to the historical figure Gamaleil. Paul himself states that he is more learned than most of his countrymen.

The Bible says: *Then Paul said: "I am a Jew, born in Tarsus of Cilicia, but brought up in this city. Under Gamaliel I was thoroughly trained in the law of our fathers and was just as zealous for God as any of you are today.* (Acts 22:3, NIV)

Though Paul was very educated, he was not beyond the spiritual or supernatural. Paul's conversion was an encounter of the luminous sort. When he attempted to convey his testimony to the king, the historical personage of Festus rebutted him.

The Bible says: *At this point Festus interrupted Paul's defense. "You are out of your mind, Paul!" he shouted. "Your great learning is driving you insane."* (Acts 26:24, NIV)

Sometimes the true intentions of the writers of the Bible get lost in the Shakespearean language and translation. We could venture to say that if Festus were speaking in modern-day vernacular, it would come across as, "Boy, you have a little bit too much edumacation. You've flipped your wig!!!"

# CHAPTER SIX

## Out of the Mouths of Babes

❧

*We have a powerful potential in our youth, and we must have the courage to change old ideas and practices so that we may direct their power toward good ends.*

—Dr. Mary McLeod Bethune

When we hear the phrase "out of the mouths of babes," we automatically think that we should really be listening to our children. After all, they might be smarter than we give them credit for. While this is a true definition of the above saying, it covers only part of the population.

How many times have we dismissed advice from someone because we felt he lacked the expertise or experience? In fact, has anyone ever not received your advice because she didn't respect your stance? We've dished out disrespect and we have been victims of it.

Yet the Bible is replete with passages about donkeys speaking and adults being led by a child. Unfortunately our prejudices preclude great sources of information coming from unexpected venues. Let's open our ears and minds to something different. Pay attention to those voices that don't matter much. You'll find that there is much to matter coming from those small voices of reason. Children do say the darndest things—but sometimes it's just what we need to hear.

*The person who knows how to laugh at himself will never cease to be amused.*

—Shirley MacLaine

## THE CHILD DELIVERER!

Being the pastor of a Full Gospel with a Pentecostal flair church, I believe in the gifts of the Spirit and the power of the Spirit. There are times in the services when I would lay hands or, should I say, two fingers on the people and they would go out in the Spirit, which means they literally would fall out as if they were asleep.

At that time some of my phrases would be "I see it, I see it, you're coming out of that." "That" could be sin, sickness, situation or disease. Or I would say, "Receive it, receive it." Now "it" could be a physical or spiritual blessing from the Lord.

They tell me when I prayed for people, I would wrinkle my nose, squint my eyes and kind of grit my teeth—who knew? Nevertheless, that's how I ministered to the people.

Well, a sister and a brother, Niah and Zay-Zay, were in the ministry. Niah had to be all of 3 years old and Zay-Zay was about 1½ years old. One day Niah got tired of her brother pooping in his diaper. So after their mother had changed his diaper, she called him and started reaching out her two fingers like she had seen me do, squinted her eyes, wrinkled her nose and grit her teeth. She told him, "Zay-Zay, lift your hands." Niah laid her two fingers on his head, and said, "Zay-Zay, you coming out of them Pampers, receive it, receive it." On cue, with no egging, prompting or assistance from any adult, he looked behind and just fell out on the floor.

**Pastor Sharon R. Robinson** leads New Jerusalem Temple of the Living God in Camden, New Jersey.

The Bible says: *And it shall come to pass, [that] whosoever shall call on the name of the LORD shall be delivered: for in mount Zion and in Jerusalem shall be deliverance, as the LORD hath said, and in the remnant whom the LORD shall call.* (Joel 2:32)

## Reflection

Deliverance. There are so many examples of deliverance in the Bible. Daniel in the lion's den. The three Hebrew boys. Paul and Silas in jail. Peter in jail. Rahab. Noah's family. The list goes on and on. But you never know how those stories or examples of deliverance will affect those around them. Albeit funny, being delivered from Pampers, it's amazing that this baby girl could realize the power of God at the age of three. Don't count anybody out. My deliverance came through the birth of a baby boy—yours can, too!

*Cultivate the habit of laughter.*

—Og Mandino

## THE WHISTLE BLOWER

My mother had a favorite necklace that she used to wear to church. It was a gold whistle that hung on a long chain. It was a gift from a very close friend.

One Sunday she and my son Khary were in church and he kept looking at the whistle. He was about four or five years old. My mom kept telling him to stop and listen quietly to the sermon. Khary kept fidgeting and finally my mom took him out to the bathroom. You know you're always in trouble when your grandma takes you to "the bathroom."

When they came back, he managed to sit quietly for a few minutes. When the pastor finished his sermon, he asked everyone to bow his or her head in prayer. The prayer included references to the sermon and ended saying, "And the trumpets blew in heaven." Well, it wasn't trumpets, just Khary, who at that very moment blew my mother's whistle very loudly. The timing was amazing. It startled quite a number of people. Possibly thinking that great and inevitable day had occurred.

Just as he was about to be chastised by my mom, one of the elderly ladies in the church said, "Barbara, don't fuss at that boy. God has sent us our own personal Gabriel."

**Karen E. Lee** is the CEO of Soul 2 Sol Public Relations in Los Angeles, California, and a member of City of Refuge Tabernacle.

The Bible says: *And the angel answering said unto him, I am Gabriel, that stand in the presence of God; and am sent to speak unto thee, and to shew thee these glad tidings.* (Luke 1:19)

*And how shall they preach, except they be sent? as it is written, How beautiful are the feet of them that preach the gospel of peace, and bring glad tidings of good things!* (Romans 10:15)

## Reflection

Gabriel. An angel and a messenger of God. It is written that the angel Gabriel told Zacharias he would be dumb until the birth of his son because he didn't believe. The angel Gabriel also told the Virgin Mary that she would give birth to the Messiah. What an awesome privilege and responsibility for God to choose those who will be His messengers. We have them among us today—pastors and preachers, evangelists and missionaries. Those who bring good tidings of great joy—words of love, peace, grace and mercy. Voices that God calls upon to carry the message that was birthed more than two thousand years ago after Gabriel was sent to a city of Galilee named Nazareth. The whistle in the hands of an innocent little boy may have shocked those who were attending service but is a great reminder of the call that has been placed upon the believer's life. So stand up, stand out and stand strong—God is on your side.

# *Laugh Stop*

### Butt Dust

A visiting minister at the start of the offertory prayer began, "Dear Lord . . ." With arms extended and a rapturous look on his upturned face, he went on, "Without you, we are but dust. . . ." He would have continued, but at the moment one very obedient little girl (who was listening carefully) leaned over to her mother and asked quite audibly in her shrill little-girl voice, "Mother, what is butt dust?" Church was pretty much over at that point. . . .

### Hello, Grandmother

One day the boss asked one of his employees, "Do you believe in life after death?" "Yes, sir," the new employee replied. "Well, then, that makes everything just fine," the boss went on. "After you left early yesterday to go to your grandmother's funeral, she stopped in to see you!"

### I Missed Jesus

It was Palm Sunday, and because of a sore throat, five-year-old Johnny stayed home from church with a sitter. When the family returned home, they were carrying several palm branches. The boy asked what they were for. "People held them over Jesus's head as he walked by." "Wouldn't you know it," the boy fumed, "the one Sunday I don't go, He shows up!"

*Always laugh when you can. It is cheap medicine.*

—Lord Byron

## GLAD TO BE IN THE SERVICE?

In this day and time, it's not uncommon that churches have more than one service during the day. The megachurch has become a staple in the Christian community, and therefore, some churches have no less than three worship services before noon.

One Sunday morning at a small church in the Midwest, a pastor noticed one of his young church members standing in the foyer staring up at a large plaque. As the pastor watched the little one, he noticed how his face got more and more intense as he read over all of the names on the wall. The plaque was covered with names with small American flags mounted on either side of it. After he had been staring at the plaque for some time, the seven-year-old started scratching his head. So the pastor walked up, stood beside the little boy and said quietly, "Good morning, Alex." "Good morning, Pastor," he replied, still focused on the plaque. Alex kept staring and staring until finally he asked, "Pastor, what is this?" The pastor said, "Well, son, it's a memorial to all the young men and women who died in the service." Soberly, they just stood together, staring at the large plaque. Finally, little Alex's voice, barely audible and trembling with fear, asked, "Which service, Pastor, the nine forty-five A.M. service or the eleven-fifteen A.M. service?"

Author unknown.

The Bible says: *With good will doing service, as to the Lord, and not to men.* (Ephesians 6:7)

## Reflection

Men and women across the United States and beyond have dedicated their lives to protecting their country. In the names of freedom and peace, they will stand on the front lines so that the liberties that we have all become used to will remain. As Christians, we should be as dedicated to the army of the Lord as those men and women who stand tall for our country. Being a soldier in the army of the Lord requires many things—from always doing the right thing, to speaking the truth in love, to doing good to those who spitefully use you to loving your enemies. There are many examples of God's soldiers, from missionaries in undeveloped countries, to the pastors who shepherd their churches to evangelists who go around the world spreading the good news of the Gospel. The best part of being a soldier in God's army is that you won't just get your name written in the Lamb's Book of Life, but you'll have an eternal home with the God of our salvation.

*A pessimist sees the difficulty in every opportunity; an optimist sees the opportunity in every difficulty.*

—Sir Winston Churchill

## WELCOME

Long before I became a pastor of a church, I made the welcome posters for my church during the last three years I was there, before I went into the Army. Anyway, I was working on the youth choir's seventh anniversary poster. I worked on this poster (by far my best work) for three hours straight. I didn't let anyone view it—though I always let my family see it in the past—to add to the surprise when it would be unveiled at the church. Being vain, I knew that once the church saw it, I would receive the appropriate attaboys and pats on the back for years to come. As I said, in the past I would show it to my family, for a reality check and an extra set of eyes to proofread—but I didn't do that and that was where I made the mistake. When I arrived at church with my chest out and back dusted off for the accolades, the poster was hoisted, hung and unfurled and that's when it was displayed for the entire world to see. It read:

WELCOE TO THE YOUTH'S CHOIR 7TH ANNIVERSARY

That's right; Mr. Senior in High School, Mr. Army-Bound, Mr. President of the Choir and Future Pastor of a Church couldn't spell, and spell-check didn't exist in 1982. Even the youngest member of the choir, all of seven years old, came by shaking her head and corrected my spelling error. The church got a good laugh and then loved on me for the rest of the concert and beyond. To tell you the truth, it really didn't hurt that much because I was with "family"! That's the difference when you are around the ones you love and you come up short—they forgive!

**Reverend Walter R. Harrison** is a pastor at Emanuel Temple in Florida.

The Bible says: *For thou, Lord, [art] good, and ready to forgive; and plenteous in mercy unto all them that call upon thee.* (Psalm 86:5).

## Reflection

We've all seen that old bumper sticker or T-shirt that states, LOVE MEANS NEVER HAVING TO SAY YOU'RE SORRY. True forgiveness may be one of mankind's greatest ways of expressing love. The act of loving the perfect, the mistake-free and the beautiful does not require significant inner strength. Not to say that it's not true love; after all, God is all those things. However, the God kind of love looks at the purposely imperfect and says, "Not only do I love you and look past your faults, but I'll do it again."

*God appoints our graces to be nurses to other men's weaknesses.*

—Henry Ward Beecher

## WHERE GRACE DWELLS

Jonathan Edward (the famous preacher) had a sister who was apparently quite a difficult woman. A potential suitor came calling one day and had apparently not heard of her nature. Edward's father attempted to talk him out of the idea. The suitor replied that he thought that she had received the grace of God so what difficulty would there be? The father's reply: "The grace of God will dwell where you or I cannot!"

**Jonathan Edwards** (1703–1758) was a colonial preacher, theologian and missionary. His famous sermon "Sinners in the Hands of an Angry God" was at the center of The Great Awakening, one of the greatest revivals in American history.

The Bible says: *Made us alive with Christ even when we were dead in transgressions—it is by grace you have been saved* (Ephesians 2:5, NIV).

## Reflection

We cannot truly fathom God's forgiveness. We question if He has forgiven us or whether He can forgive the atrocities of various individuals we see as villains. It appears that only His grace will go where "even the angels fear to tread." This also applies to those who are in our lives who may be difficult to live with. To know that God's grace can even abide with them is also knowing His grace will live with us through our difficult times.

# *Laugh Stop*

## Under Five

A little boy in church for the first time watched as the ushers passed around the offering plates. When they came near his pew, the boy said loudly, "Don't pay for me, Daddy, I'm under five."

## I Can't Pray???

After being interviewed by the school administration, the teaching prospect said, "Let me see if I've got this right: You want me to go into that room with all those kids, correct their disruptive behavior, observe them for signs of abuse, monitor their dress habits, censor their T-shirt messages and instill in them a love for learning. You want me to check their backpacks for weapons, wage war on drugs and sexually transmitted diseases and raise their sense of self-esteem and personal pride. You want me to teach them patriotism and good citizenship, sportsmanship and fair play, and how to register to vote, balance a checkbook and apply for a job. You want me to check their heads for lice, recognize signs of antisocial behavior and make sure that they all pass the state exams. You want me to provide them with an equal education regardless of their handicaps, and communicate regularly with their parents by letter, telephone, newsletter and report card. You want me to do all this with a piece of chalk, a blackboard, a bulletin board, a few books, a big smile and a starting salary that qualifies me for food stamps. You want me to do all this and then you tell me . . . I CAN'T PRAY?"

*At the height of laughter, the universe is flung into a kaleidoscope of new possibilities.*

—Jean Houston

## THE BURNING HAIR

One thing I love about the Catholic faith is its people's reverence for God. When you go into most Catholic churches, it is so quiet and so serene. When I was in high school, friends of mine who were Catholic came to my church for a youth choir concert we were having. I was so excited they were there until I saw a look of horror on their faces while sitting on the back pew. So I went back to ask them what was wrong. My friend Lisa said, "I can't believe you guys are talking—we would be slapped one thousand times if we talked at church."

My friend Tracie Mayer told me her story about a time at her Catholic school when she was in the fourth grade and was nine years old. As she recalls . . .

Going into Our Lady of Mount Virgin Church during recess or at any other time unsupervised was tantamount to a sin. A big one. But as the other kids hollered and jumped rope and kicked balls and played tetherball, my girlfriend and I decided that we would quietly escape the school grounds and slip through the weighty doors of the church and ascend the stairs.

We only wanted to light a couple of candles and give them up as offering.

I shall never forget the sheath of albino white fright on the face of my girlfriend JoAnne, nor the way she looked at my face, opened her mouth and started screaming. I guess a nine-year-old shouldn't play with matches—or if she does, she'd better know what she's doing. Along with the smell of burning candles, I also started to smell singed hair—suddenly the shock of my burning hair propelled me into movement. As I flailed my hands this way and that at my head, JoAnne suddenly unfroze and began helping me extinguish the flames that had jumped to my head apparently. I whipped my arm this way and that way to do whatever I could to extinguish my hair flame. I won't even tell you what trouble I got into. But they say a girl's hair is her crowning glory. Well, that evening, my crowning glory was gone when my dad cut off what was left of my mid-back-length hair into something similar to a crew cut. My hair never grew to that length again!

**Tracie Mayer** is a loving mother and wife who resides in Germany.

The Bible says: *Then Jesus six days before the Passover came to Bethany, where Lazarus was, which had been dead, whom he raised from the dead. There they made him a supper; and Martha served: but Lazarus was one of them that sat at the table with him. Then took Mary a pound of ointment of spikenard, very costly, and anointed the feet of Jesus, and wiped his feet with her hair: and the house was filled with the odour of the ointment. Then saith one of his disciples, Judas Iscariot, Simon's [son], which should betray him, Why was not this ointment sold for three hundred pence, and given to the poor? This he said, not that he cared for the poor; but because he was a thief, and had the bag, and bare what was put therein. Then said Jesus, Let her alone: against the day of my burying hath she kept this. For the poor always ye have with you; but me ye have not always. (John 12:1–8)*

## Reflection

It has been said that a woman's hair is her crowning glory. Women are real particular when it comes to their hair. Anybody who knows me knows that I pride myself in always having my hair together. If it's not together, then I'm either sick or my hairstylist wasn't available. But this story of a woman who used her hair to dry Jesus's feet is both priceless and precious. She used an ointment that equated to (in that time) three hundred days of labor or almost a year's salary. However, Mary's willingness to forfeit financial gain speaks volumes to the deep devotion she had for her Lord. Never be afraid to use what you have, whether great or small, to let God know that you love, adore and value Him.

*People see God every day, they just don't recognize Him.*

—Pearl Bailey

## THE STORY OF NOAH

When I was growing up, my church, like most, had Sunday School. The difference was we had ours on Saturday and we called it Sabbath School. So every Saturday, the church doors would open and classes would begin, separated by ages—Nursery Class, Middle School, Teens, Young Adults and Adults. Now, I wasn't in this class then, but I've been told over and over about a Sabbath School lesson that had the church roaring with laughter.

One of our beloved church members was a woman named Alma Brown. We all called her Cousin Alma (to this day I'm not sure if she really was related). But she was a strong woman of faith, dedicated to God and unwavering when it came to what God can do. Whenever a situation arose, her FIRST thought was prayer. There was no doubt about it. Let me give you an example. One Saturday afternoon I was having a little, let's say, constipation problem in the bathroom. I must have been about eight years old. While I was in the bathroom, Cousin Alma came in and must have heard my "discomfort" and asked me what was wrong. I told her I was having a little problem and immediately she went to prayer: "Lord, help her, Jesus!

Help her! Send her some release and relief in Jesus's name!" As I sat there, I couldn't believe what I was hearing . . . somebody praying for my relief? But as a grown woman, I now see that her faith was so strong and she went to God for everything, so her first thought was to pray. Nothing else came to mind. What a great example of faith and trust.

Now back to Sabbath School. Well, Cousin Alma was not a young woman—when I was young, I'd venture to say she was at least seventy years old. But she knew the Bible and was a great teacher! So this particular Saturday, she was teaching the kids the story of Noah. She was sharing Noah's faith and what God had called him to do. She told the story of the building of the ark and the animals that were called to come in, both male and female. She talked about Noah preaching for years and years and years. As she was sharing the story with such passion and vigor, one of the young kids yelled out, "Were you there?????"

**Patti S. Webster** is the CEO of W&W Public Relations, Inc., and a member of Shiloh Pentecostal Church, Inc.-Christian Love Center in Somerville, New Jersey.

The Bible says: *Not slothful in business; fervent in spirit; serving the Lord.* (Romans 12:11)

### Reflection

When I read this story, I think of the old hymn that goes something like this:

*Were you there when they crucified my Lord?*
*Were you there when they crucified my Lord?*
*Oh!*
*Sometimes it causes me to tremble, tremble, tremble.*
*Were you there when they crucified my Lord?*

Although funny, Cousin Alma was so impassioned by the Word of God, her fervency was displayed in her speech, in her actions and in her life. She was a true example of how we should be. Boldly proclaiming the things of God, not ashamed of the Gospel of Jesus Christ. How amazing is it that she was so ignited by the Word that a young child would think that she lived two thousand years ago. What happens when we share the Word of God with friends and family? Are we so ignited that they, too, catch on fire? Or are we so dull and boring that those who are listening fall asleep? And what about her faith? Granted, it was a little embarrassing having someone praying for you in the bathroom—and Lord knows who came in and wondered what was going on. But it obviously affected my life because I've never forgotten what she did. As I know she is now resting at heaven's door, I pray my life will touch someone just as hers touched mine.

# *Laugh Stop*

### Forgive Your Enemies

Toward the end of Sunday service, the minister asked, "How many of you have forgiven your enemies?" Eighty percent held up their hands. The minister then repeated his question. All responded this time, except one small elderly lady. "Mrs. Jones? Are you not willing to forgive your enemies?" "I don't have any," she replied, smiling sweetly. "Mrs. Jones, that is very unusual. How old are you?" "Ninety-eight," she replied. "Oh, Mrs. Jones, would you please come down in front and tell us all how a person can live ninety-eight years and not have an enemy in the world?" The little sweetheart of a lady tottered down the aisle, faced the congregation and said: "I outlived them all!"

### Three Hymns

One Sunday a pastor told the congregation that the church needed some extra money and asked the people to prayerfully consider giving a little extra in the offering plate. He said that whoever gave the most would be able to pick out three hymns. After the offering plates were passed, the pastor glanced down and noticed that someone had placed a thousand-dollar bill in the offering. He was so excited that he immediately shared his joy with his congregation and said he'd like to personally thank the person who placed the money in the plate. A very quiet, elderly and saintly lady all the way in the back shyly raised her hand. The pastor asked her to come to the front. Slowly she made her way to the pastor. He told her how wonderful it was that she gave so much and in thanksgiving asked her to pick out three hymns. Her eyes brightened as she looked over the congregation, pointed to the three handsomest men in the building and said, "I'll take him and him and him."

*The hardest job kids face today is learning good manners without ever seeing any.*

—Fred Astaire

## WHO DO YOU WANT TO BE?

Kids really do say the dandiest things—but sometimes you just don't want to have them say them in church! Let me explain.

There were two sisters in my church named the Harris sisters. Cool girls, lots of fun—but they were bad. The older sister had a baby daughter named Tasha. Tasha was bad. There was just badness in their blood. So here comes Easter Sunday. Our church put together a really great Easter program—plays, recitations, Easter songs—you name it, we did it. Everyone was excited to be able to get dressed in his or her Easter finest— showing off new shoes and new dresses and hats. As all this was on Easter Sunday, it also gave the parents bragging rights as their kids intoned Easter poems or recitations.

Well, the Harris sisters were coaching Tasha and were excited that she was finally prepared to present her Easter recitation. Tasha was just two years old. Tasha flawlessly performed her recitation. As she was standing there, the Sunday School teacher asked her, "What do you want to be when you grow up, Tasha?" Tasha looked at her and said, "The devil!" It took a whole lot of smelling salts to wake up the church mothers who simultaneously passed out!

**Tichina Arnold** is an award-winning actress best known for her role as Pam on *Martin*. She currently plays the lead role on *Everybody Hates Chris*, the highly successful television series based on the life of comedian Chris Rock.

The Bible says: *Train up a child in the way he should go: and when he is old, he will not depart from it.* (Proverbs 22:6)

## Reflection

Children, much of the time, speak what truly is in their hearts. That is, unless they've stolen the cookies or broken the vase. Outside of these types of things they are prone to say things we wished they hadn't said. Much of the time it's things we've said and wished they hadn't heard. The problem is not that we don't teach our children right and wrong. It's that we teach them that right is good but bad is better with our actions and examples.

*Managing to have a sense of humor makes it a lot eas-
ier to manage people.*

—Steve Wilson

## BAPTIZE ME SLOWLY

My sons had made the decision to be baptized after we recently joined our new church. My youngest son has a wonderful sense of humor and he was a little scared of being submerged
under water. At first he asked the pastor to say his full name
(a convenient stall tactic) and then he told the pastor, "Now,
do it slowly." Since the pastor had a microphone on, the whole
church heard him and the congregation erupted into laughter.
Our pastor was so good with him he said "That's right, Jordan,
you want to make sure that I take my time and do it slowly
and that's what I am going to do."

**Kenneth A. Myles** is a native of Saginaw, Michigan, and
is employed by Procter & Gamble in Cincinnati, Ohio. He
serves as a board member for Greater Cincinnati Behavioral
Health Services and is president and CEO of KAMJAM Entertainment. **Sonia J. Myles,** also a native of Saginaw, Michigan, is the director of Global Media Purchases for Procter &
Gamble and serves as a board member for Impact Young
Lives, Women Helping Women, and as the advisory board

chair for Florida A&M University's School of Business and Industry (her alma mater). They are the proud parents of Kendall, twelve, and Jordan, ten. Sonia is currently completing her first book, entitled *7 Spirit-Filled Strategies for Raising a Loving Child.*

The Bible says: *Finally, [be ye] all of one mind, having compassion one of another, love as brethren, [be] pitiful, [be] courteous.* (I Peter 3:8)

## Reflection

In the innocence of a child's fearful words, we can see great compassion from Jordan's pastor. And because of his compassion, I'm sure that quelled Jordan's fears of being submerged in the water. The Bible teaches us to have compassion for one another. And there are many examples given of Jesus's great compassion for those who were sick, or in distress or demonized. The Word tells us of the father who had great compassion for a prodigal son. There's also a story about the Good Samaritan who helped a brother in need when he found him on the side of the road. Let compassion rule in your hearts, my friend. Look for opportunities in your community, at your job, at your church to show you have concern for others. A compassionate heart can only lead to good things and changed lives.

# Humor in the Bible

## Be Careful of What You Pray for; You Might Get It

Prayer to many of us seems like a futile effort and a last-ditch attempt at hope. We pray, but really don't believe that the receiving part is viable. Why else are we shocked when that inevitable answer to our prayers takes place? It's like, "Oh my gosh, this prayer stuff really works." I can imagine the shock, the excitement and the little bit of fear felt by the young woman named Rhoda in the book of Acts.

The Bible says: *It was about this time that King Herod arrested some who belonged to the church, intending to persecute them. He had James, the brother of John, put to death with the sword. When he saw that this pleased the Jews, he proceeded to seize Peter also. This happened during the Feast of Unleavened Bread. After arresting him, he put him in prison, handing him over to be guarded by four squads of four soldiers each. Herod intended to bring him out for public trial after the Passover. So Peter was kept in prison, but the church was earnestly praying to God for him. The night before Herod was to bring him to trial,*

*Peter was sleeping between two soldiers, bound with two chains, and sentries stood guard at the entrance. Suddenly an angel of the Lord appeared and a light shone in the cell. He struck Peter on the side and woke him up. "Quick, get up!" he said, and the chains fell off Peter's wrists. Then the angel said to him, "Put on your clothes and sandals." And Peter did so. "Wrap your cloak around you and follow me," the angel told him. Peter followed him out of the prison, but he had no idea that what the angel was doing was really happening; he thought he was seeing a vision. They passed the first and second guards and came to the iron gate leading to the city. It opened for them by itself, and they went through it. When they had walked the length of one street, suddenly the angel left him. Then Peter came to himself and said, "Now I know without a doubt that the Lord sent his angel and rescued me from Herod's clutches and from everything the Jewish people were anticipating." When this had dawned on him, he went to the house of Mary the mother of John, also called Mark, where many people had gathered and were praying. Peter knocked at the outer entrance, and a servant girl named Rhoda came to answer the door. When she recognized Peter's voice, she was so overjoyed she ran back without opening it and exclaimed, "Peter is at the door!"* (Acts 12:12–14, NIV)

Of course, initially she did not think it was the answer to her and her companions' prayers, but an apparition or the ghost or spirit of Peter. It's amazing how a little fright can bring out the rudeness in most of us. Just look at how she slams the door in Peter's face. Apparently Peter wasn't offended. I can't imagine a smile didn't crack on his face as he awaited an invite into the house. Many of us today want to hear from God—just not the actual voice.

## IS THIS BIG ENOUGH FOR YOU?

One vehicle for humor in the Bible is sarcasm. Sometimes it's done humorously. Sometimes it's done caustically. No individual in the Bible uses this more than Paul. Sarcasm within itself is not necessarily considered nice. However, what makes us laugh is the unexpected anecdote. What is more unexpected than our orthodox Paul being a smarty? This aspect of his personality has been covered and overlooked for two millennia because of religiosity and tradition. To see this sarcasm of Paul, we will have to reinterpret how we've looked at certain passages that we've read, in some cases, since childhood.

Those who are intelligent often use sarcasm, for all it's worth. The use of their sarcasm, though, might not be good evidence of their intelligence quotient. More often it is used to show the intended how idiotic they must be for not getting the point.

A few of Paul's sarcastic remarks will require a bit of explanation, as the humor is not immediately apparent. In the majority of his writings, he uses a secretary. This was common practice in those days as even the literate rarely wrote at length and their penmanship left much to be desired. Though they may have been highly learned, writing material was also not in abundant supply. Subsequently, the practice of writing was not so readily available. Paul was no different, even at his advanced knowledge and intelligence.

The Galatians were initially offspring of Paul's missionary activities. One in which he took great pride. Eventually they succumbed to a much more conservative and strict branch of the newfound Christian faith. These followers enforced more of the practices and ritual ceremonies of the Jewish faith in the past. One of these practices was the circumcision. A strong prerequisite for adherence of the Old Testament law. Obviously this procedure did not fly too well with many Christians who had come from a non-Jewish background. Many decided simply not to follow this new faith. Others reluctantly agreed. This upset Paul and he wondered aloud what caused them to defect from his teaching.

As he is about to close the letter to these Galatians, he grabs the pen away from his scribe and writes in his own autograph.

The Bible says: *See what large letters I use as I write to you with my own hand!* (Galatians 6:11, NIV)

I can imagine Paul went, "Give me this pen. I'll show 'em!" Of course, there is more sarcasm from Paul. Before he facetiously asked them to see his large handwriting, he went to a previous sarcastic depth.

# CHAPTER SEVEN

## Three Weddings and a Funeral

*A successful marriage requires falling in love many times,
always with the same person.*

—Germaine Greer

Death and life are in the power of the tongue. This is what our Bible tells us. Of course without getting too much into hermeneutics, we can declare that this is literal or figurative speech. Yet no one can disagree that the words and actions we state can have a profound effect on all of us.

One of the most precious institutions that was ever designed by God is marriage. For some, it will be the day when you stand face-to-face with your true love and declare your undying devotion and commitment to each other and a new life begins. But after the pomp, circumstance, flowers and bridal party, reality sets in. You realize that Mr. Right isn't perfect and Mrs. Right isn't necessarily just what the doctor ordered. Marriage almost always leads to humorous scenarios in one's life—it can't be avoided. From his leaving his clothes on the floor to her loud snoring to his mother being a busybody to her girlfriends getting into their business and giving bad advice. It's also a place where movie and television producers can find their most honest stories.

For all of us, death is inevitable and it can have the most profound effect on one's life. I've personally experienced a lot of death in my life. There was one year that I couldn't understand what God was doing because it seemed like every couple of weeks someone else I knew had died. It's not always at the happiest moments in my life, like at a wedding, that some of the funniest things happen, but also at some of the saddest moments in my life. These stories show that in life and in death, laughter can still be a healing balm.

In this light, let's keep in mind how we treat one another. Let it be with the love of Christ. Use words that uplift rather than bring down. All we need to do is pause and pray at those times when the wrong words are trying to come out. Then subsequently do the right actions that can bring love and happiness.

We won't be perfect. However, you'll find that you'll do better in bringing about three weddings to every one funeral.

*There is, hidden or flaunted, a sword between the sexes*
*till an entire marriage reconciles them.*

—C.S. Lewis

## HELP ME, DAVE

During a recent interview with Reverend Robert Schuller on his Hour of Power program, Pastor Schuller asked Joyce Meyer about her meeting her husband, Dave.

JOYCE MEYER: And then I met the man that I've been married to now for thirty-nine-and-a-half years who's . . .

ROBERT SCHULLER: That's great. He's here; stand up.

JOYCE MEYER: . . . sitting out here today. Dave.

ROBERT SCHULLER: That's another very powerful reason why
you have this successful ministry you have.

JOYCE MEYER: Yes, exactly.

ROBERT SCHULLER: Absolutely. My spouse is my biggest
asset.

JOYCE MEYER: Well, Dave was a Christian and he was praying for a wife. He was twenty-six years old and he'd been
asking God to give him a wife. It was time to get married. And he said make it someone who needs help.

ROBERT SCHULLER: (Laughs.)

JOYCE MEYER: And believe me, I needed a lot of help.

**Joyce Meyer** is a popular Christian author and speaker.
Her television and radio programs air in twenty-five languages
in two hundred countries, and she has written over seventy
books on Christianity.

The Bible says: *He who finds a wife finds what is good
and receives favor from the LORD.* (Proverbs 18:22, NIV)

## Reflection

While driving down a highway, a Christian couple observed
two elderly women experiencing a flat tire. They decided to
circle around to assist the women. By the time they got to the

women's car, a young man on a bicycle had pulled over to give them a hand. It was apparent that the young man was slightly mentally handicapped. The husband got out of his car to observe the young man change the tire. The man was successful. The elderly women gave him about five dollars for assisting them. However, "It could have been a million dollars and it still would have paled compared to the pride the young man had in being able to help someone," the husband stated. This is the reward we all should desire. Not the wealth, but the overwhelming feeling of humanity that God gives us when we help others.

*Laughter is the closest distance between two people.*

—Victor Borge

## SOMEONE'S TRYING TO HOLD ME DOWN!

During a baptism ceremony one of our congregants decided it was time for him to get serious and get baptized. In the past he had been not so nice to his sweet wife, sometimes blaming her for some of his shortcomings. The baptismal pool was located in the basement of this eighty-year-old church. Due to the age of the building and the location of the baptismal pool, there were loose boards and things that occasionally hooked on to articles of clothing.

Eventually it was the husband's turn to make his way to the pool. As he got up to walk toward the pastor, his gown caught hold of something. He acted nonchalant as he pretended nothing was wrong. It soon became all too apparent that something had snagged on to him and wouldn't let go. He stopped and paused when he heard a slight tear. Not wanting to expose the real him, he stopped and pulled the garment from the nail. Without missing a beat, the husband looked at his wife, then at the rest of the congregants and said, "See, she's even trying to stop me from getting baptized."

The candidates were led into a back room, where they clothed themselves in baptism robes. The ceremony took some time as the crowded basement had a small worship service to accompany the baptisms.

After the laughter had died down and he approached the pool, he gave one more look at his wife and she at him as they shared that look of love that only a husband and wife can.

Author unknown.

The Bible says: *At that hour of the night the jailer took them and washed their wounds; then immediately he and all his family were baptized. The jailer brought them into his house and set a meal before them; he was filled with joy because he had come to believe in God—he and his whole family.* (Acts 16:33–34, NIV)

## Reflection

The silver lining mythically believed to be part of every dark cloud is not so difficult to find as we may think. The problem lies in the seeker.

*Marriage is the perfection of what love aimed at, ignorant of what it sought.*

—Ralph Waldo Emerson

## THE SWEET SMELL OF MATRIMONY

I was visiting a church, and a guest preacher touched on the topic of marriage. She told the congregation how she'd met her husband at the age of sixty-eight. She was now seventy-eight, and let me tell you she was gorgeous and didn't look like she was older than fifty-five. She preached, "God blessed me with my husband. I met him in the supermarket and he is twenty years my junior. We have been so happy, thanks to God's blessing. I was also wearing my very special eau de toilette. Don't worry, ladies, I have some on sale right outside for just five dollars a bottle and it really works!" She brought her handsome husband to the altar to show the congregation how happy they were in matrimony. Before you knew it, all you heard was a stampede of high heels as women peeled themselves from the pews even before she finished her sermon to buy their very own bottle!

**Laura Santiago** is a brand manager in the beauty industry in New York City. She loves the Lord and to this day still has her eau de toilette, but is still single and waiting for God to bestow upon her the man He has planned for her.

The Bible says: *But I am afraid that just as Eve was deceived by the serpent's cunning, your minds may somehow be led astray from your sincere and pure devotion to Christ.* (2 Corinthians 11:3)

## Reflection

We all want to be loved; that is a pretty honest statement across the board. I don't believe there is a person living who doesn't want to know they are special and loved and have a place in this world and in someone's heart. As a single woman, I also understand the desire to be married. The world shouts out the word "MARRIAGE" all the time. The world says you are incomplete without a mate. I disagree! True completeness comes when you fall in love with Jesus Christ. The single life can be a bit discouraging for single Christians at times. That's just real. You get lonely, you get discouraged and you have sexual thoughts. Right? But I've made it through the singles cycle, and I'm learning to be content in whatever state I'm in, so what now? You have to ask yourself the question, "What can I do to be single and satisfied because of Christ?" Here are a few helpful hints:

1. Live each day for God;
2. Seek always to know more about God;
3. Seize opportunities to help others;
4. Go places, rather than sit at home, waiting to be discovered; travel;

5.  Spend personal time on self-improvement;

6.  Bravely establish a faith in God that affirms your ability to make it in life;

7.  Focus on the goodness of God and be grateful;

8.  Don't get obsessed with singleness in your prayer life;

9.  Stomp on the flesh. Be very careful about your thought life and about the movie theater of your mind;

10. Keep so busy that misery hasn't got a chance to get in. The worst times are when you are idle. Laziness is an enemy of the soul;

11. Love your church and be active;

12. Don't play games and don't be devastated if people try to play matchmaker for you or start rumors;

13. Prize the friendships you do have and work on them, as they can be richly rewarding;

14. Be open. The man God has for you may be a garbage-man, a tax collector or a teacher, not necessarily an NBA superstar or a knight in shining armor. He may also be fifteen years younger than you. Don't push away God's perfect will for your life and don't be so set in your ways that you miss the one person who will complement you—spiritually, physically, emotionally and financially.

Live your life according to Matthew 6:33: *But seek ye first the kingdom of God, and His righteousness and all these things* [emphasis mine: everything your heart desires according to His will] *shall be added unto you.*

# *Laugh Stop*

### The End Is Near

A local priest and rabbi were fishing on the side of the road. They thoughtfully made a sign saying, THE END IS NEAR! TURN YOURSELF AROUND NOW BEFORE IT'S TOO LATE! and showed it to each passing car. One person who drove by didn't appreciate the sign and shouted at them, "Leave us alone, you religious nuts!" All of a sudden they heard a big splash. They looked at each other and the priest said to the rabbi, "You think we should just put up a sign that says BRIDGE OUT instead?"

### Marble Not

Because they believe the Word of God, young kids were told they couldn't play with marbles because the Bible said, "Marble not!"

### Hell Is Full?

A college drama group presented a play in which one character would stand on a trap door and announce, "I descend into hell!" A stagehand below would then pull a rope, the trap door would spring and the actor would drop from view. The play was well received. When the actor playing the part became ill, another actor who was quite overweight took his place. When the new actor announced, "I descend into hell!" the stagehand pulled the rope, and the actor began his plunge, but became hopelessly stuck. No amount of tugging on the rope could make him descend. One student in the balcony jumped up and yelled: "Hallelujah! Hell is full!"

*Laugh alone and the world thinks you're an idiot!*

—Anonymous

## I'M ALIVE!

It was a sad day this Saturday morning as a family was burying their son. Death is inevitable for all of us, and the somberness of a funeral is, for lack of a better word, grave.

So on this day, the normal program took place: the processional, followed by a congregational hymn, followed by the Old Testament and New Testament scripture, followed by the choir song, followed by the reading of the obituary. As the church secretary came to read the obituary, everyone in the service read along with her. So she began with the birth of the young man and lovingly read about his life. As she neared the end, she started to read a list of his surviving family members and those who had predeceased him, including one of his uncles. As she read the names, all of a sudden, out of the crowd, a voice said, "I'm alive! I'm alive!" One of the family members who was mistaken for dead was actually alive and in the service to mourn the death of his nephew.

No one wants to laugh at a funeral—that's not the most appropriate time or place—but can you imagine the silent tears of laughter as the voice in the crowd barreled through this solemn assembly to proclaim that there was, indeed, life in the man's body! One is left to wonder if he checked his pulse to make sure.

**Gerrod White** is the minister of music at Shiloh Pentecostal Church, Inc.–Christian Love Center in Somerville, New Jersey, and the Chicago Bulls' biggest fan.

The Bible says: *But I would not have you to be ignorant, brethren, concerning them which are asleep, that ye sorrow not, even as others which have no hope. For if we believe that Jesus died and rose again, even so them also which sleep in Jesus will God bring with him. For this we say unto you by the word of the Lord, that we which are alive [and] remain unto the coming of the Lord shall not prevent them which are asleep. For the Lord himself shall descend from heaven with a shout, with the voice of the archangel, and with the trump of God: and the dead in Christ shall rise first: Then we which are alive [and] remain shall be caught up together with them in the clouds, to meet the Lord in the air: and so shall we ever be with the Lord. Wherefore comfort one another with these words.* (I Thessalonians 4:11–18)

## Reflection

Death is never easy. I've had so much death in my life. From my grandparents to one of my best friends who died before the age of thirty-two. There was a year when I felt like all I was doing was going to funerals. I couldn't understand how God could take friends who had barely lived their life, or people who appeared to be the picture of health. But I realize that those who believe in God don't have to mourn as others mourn. Those who believe in God have a hope beyond this world. And a time to weep will become a time to laugh and a time to mourn will become a time to dance.

*I'm a great believer in luck, and I find the harder I
work, the more I have of it.*

—Thomas Jefferson

## CHINESE HORSES

One of Dr. Robert Schuller's favorite stories is the classic
tale of the Chinese man who had one horse and one son. One
day his horse broke out of the corral and fled to the freedom of
the hills. The neighbors came around that night and chattered,
"Your horse got out? What bad luck!"

"Why?" the old Chinese man said. "How do you know it's
bad luck?" Sure enough, the next night the horse came back to
his familiar corral for his usual feeding and watering, leading
twelve wild stallions with him. The farmer's son saw the thirteen horses in the corral, slipped out and locked the gate. Suddenly, he had thirteen horses instead of none.

The neighbors heard the good news and came chattering to
the farmer, "Oh, you have thirteen horses. What good luck!"
The old Chinese man answered, "How do you know that's good
luck?" Some days later, his strong young son was trying to
break one of the wild stallions only to be thrown off and have
his leg broken. The neighbors came back that night and passed
another hasty judgment. "Your son broke his leg? What bad
luck." And the wise farmer answered again, "How do you know
it's bad luck?'

Sure enough, a few days later, a Chinese warlord came through town and conscripted every able-bodied young man, taking them off to war, never to return again. But the young man was saved because of his broken leg. Only God knows what's good for us and what's bad for us.

**Pastor Robert Harold Schuller** is an American televangelist and pastor known around the world through his weekly *Hour of Power* television program. His Crystal Cathedral in Garden Grove, California, is world renowned for being able to accommodate those in their cars, much like a drive-in theater. He is also the author of over sixty books.

The Bible says: *For we must all appear before the judgment seat of Christ, that each one may receive what is due him for the things done while in the body, whether good or bad.* (2 Corinthians 5:10, NIV)

## Reflection

Our lives appear to have those things happen to us that many would say we don't deserve. These can be good things and these can be bad things. Often luck is the attributing factor, in many people's opinion. Some would argue that good luck takes away two things. The first would be the hard work it took to get the accomplishment. The second thing "good luck" takes away is God's hand of grace and mercy. Bad luck simply takes God out completely.

# *Laugh Stop*

### Hallelujah and Praise the Lord

A poor man came into a small town out West, and while looking for some kind of help, he went to one of the local churches. He was greeted by the pastor who, when hearing of the poor man's troubles, decided to feed and clothe him. Much to the man's surprise, the pastor even decided to provide him with a donkey and some additional items to help him on his journey. "But," warned the pastor, "I must tell you that to make the donkey go, you have to say 'Hallelujah,' and then to make the donkey stop, you must say 'Amen.' If you remember that, you'll be fine." The poor man graciously thanked the preacher, mounted the donkey and continued his journey. As the sun began to set, he decided to stop the donkey and find a place to rest. But the only problem was, he couldn't remember how to stop the donkey! The donkey kept going on for another ten minutes or so, until they started to get near a dangerous cliff. Now the man started getting nervous. He tried almost everything to get the donkey to stop, but it would not. He finally decided to pray to God to save him. He ended the prayer by saying "Amen" out loud, and the donkey stopped just right on the edge of the cliff. Had he waited one second more, he would have fallen off the cliff to his doom. When he saw that the donkey had stopped, he shouted out in joy, "Hallelujah!" . . .

*I believe that imagination is stronger than knowledge—myth is more potent than history—dreams are more powerful than facts—hope always triumphs over experience—laughter is the cure for grief—love is stronger than death.*

—Robert Fulghum

## MY GRANDMOTHER VATUS

I have the most amazing family. Funny. Loving. Caring. Large. And on both sides, my grandparents were totally dedicated to making sure that the family glue was strong and the foundation was God. And it still is. I tell people all the time that we are truly the family from Soul Food, eating together, hanging out together, working together and serving God together. And one of the key reasons why we are so connected is my grandmother, Vatus Webster.

Grandma was something else. She used to tell us that when "death came knocking at her door, she wasn't going to be home." HILARIOUS! This is also the woman who would visit for a long weekend carrying only a small duffel bag that was about a foot long. I could never figure out how she could get four dresses, shoes, underwear, stockings and toiletries in that little bag. And Grandma was the reporter of the family. If you wanted to know what was going on with ANYONE in the family, you just called Grandma. But you knew that when you called her, the line would be busy because she refused to get call waiting. So, you had to keep calling her back. She knew where everyone was, what he or she was doing and not doing (like calling or visiting her), and she never forgot a birthday. Grandma was filled with life, laughter—she was just a funny woman.

So when diabetes hit her and she had to get her leg amputated, I wasn't surprised that she took it all in stride. All she'd say was, "God has been good to me." I couldn't have asked for a better example of God's love.

Then on September 5, 1999, the Lord finally called Grandma home for her great and deserving reward. She had buried two children before her plus her husband, and I believe that when my Uncle Daniel died, she didn't want to go through that again. She wanted to die before the rest of her children. Just my thoughts. In any case, the family made preparations for her funeral, which was held at Reid's Temple Church of God in Christ, where she was a lifelong member and church mother. At the funeral, I was not surprised that it was overflowing with well-wishers, her church family, our family (which had to be 150 people) and the members of Reid's church. Mother Vatus (as they called her) was dedicated to the ministry and always had an encouraging word for everyone.

As I reflect, I can clearly remember the day of her funeral. I was sitting in the midst of our family, of course quiet, somber and tearful. And as is protocol at a funeral, someone was set to read Grandma's obituary. I can't remember who, but as she was reading the obituary, I heard her say my grandmother's name wrong, which wasn't a big deal because Vatus (pronounced VAY-TUSS) isn't a common name. As she continued reading, she said her name wrong again—"VAT-US." And again, I heard "VAT-US." She just KNEW she was saying her name right. After the fourth time, I was getting a little mad that this woman was defaming my grandmother's good name. But then I looked up and saw the shoulders of my Uncle Leroy going up and down—he was laughing. So I started to laugh. And laugh. And laugh. This was so Grandma—at what was one of the saddest days of my life, laughter would creep in. She loved laughter—she would laugh at the simplest things. So in her honor, I said good-bye with a mouthful of laughter, tears in my eyes and a smile on my face.

**Patti S. Webster** is the CEO of W&W Public Relations, Inc., and a member of Shiloh Pentecostal Church, Inc.–Christian Love Center in Somerville, New Jersey.

The Bible says: *Now also when I am old and grayheaded, O God, forsake me not; until I have shewed thy strength unto [this] generation, [and] thy power to every one [that] is to come.* (Psalm 71:18)

*We will not hide [them] from their children, shewing to the generation to come the praises of the LORD, and his strength, and his wonderful works that he hath done.* (Psalm 78:4)

*That the generation to come might know [them, even] the children [which] should be born; [who] should arise and declare [them] to their children.* (Psalm 78:6)

## Reflection

Enjoy your family. Laugh with your family. Love your family. Cherish your family. They are your most valuable commodities.

# Humor in the Bible

## Take My Wife, Please

"Take my wife, please." So goes the famous punch line of Henny Youngman. Husband and wife jokes are as old and older than vaudeville. While the Bible does not tell actual jokes, it does have humor imbedded in certain statements, and many would find it difficult to believe that humor wasn't an intended element.

Most of these spousal jokes, primarily targeting the women (sorry, ladies), are found in Proverbs and are probably the result of a man with too many women. Uh . . . Solomon.

The Bible says: *Better to live on a corner of the roof than share a house with a quarrelsome wife.* (Proverbs 21:9, NIV)

The Bible says: *Better to live in a desert than with a quarrelsome and ill-tempered wife.* (Proverbs 21:19, NIV)

According to Solomon here, considered one of the wisest men to have ever lived, it doesn't really matter where one lives— whether a desert or the corner of a roof—as long as it's not in the same house as either an argumentative or an ill-tempered wife. This statement, of course, might make some women argumentative or ill tempered.

The Bible says: *A quarrelsome wife is like a constant dripping on a rainy day.* (Proverbs 27:15, NIV)

The Bible says: *A foolish son is his father's ruin, and a quarrelsome wife is like constant dripping.* (Proverbs 19:3, NIV)

Most mainstream Christian and Jewish scholars believe Solomon wrote most of the Proverbs. Many who have read the Bible know of Solomon's reputation with women.

Calling one's wife a drip might not fly over too well. But it sure is funny stuff.

## Jesus Is Here; Better Get Dressed

The unexpected visitor has caused many of us to scramble for something to wear. When nothing is available, we are often seen peeking around the door explaining to our little intruder that it will be a moment. What would you do if Jesus unexpectedly wrung the bell?

The Bible says: *Early in the morning, Jesus stood on the shore, but the disciples did not realize that it was Jesus. He called out to them, "Friends, haven't you any fish?" "No,"*

*they answered. He said, "Throw your net on the right side*
*of the boat and you will find some." When they did, they*
*were unable to haul the net in because of the large number*
*of fish. Then the disciple whom Jesus loved said to Peter,*
*"It is the Lord!" As soon as Simon Peter heard him say,*
*"It is the Lord," he wrapped his outer garment around*
*him (for he had taken it off) and jumped into the water.*
*The other disciples followed in the boat, towing the net full*
*of fish, for they were not far from shore, about a hundred*
*yards. When they landed, they saw a fire of burning coals*
*there with fish on it, and some bread.* (John 21:4–9, NIV)

Peter is so excited he puts on "his clothes" to go swimming.
Why wrap up in something if you're still going to jump in the
water?! The stuff is too hilarious to be made up.

Kind of reminds you of Adam, his predecessor of about four
thousand years, and his attempt at covering his nakedness. You
have to wonder what made Peter's nakedness so embarrassing
that he had to jump ship to hide it. Of course, this was after
the resurrection, and having his all-and-all exposed for the Lord
of Glory is not the most comfortable situation to be in. Regardless of His understanding.

## Abraham and Sarah Are Having a Baby

This may be the story most experienced students of the
Bible will go to in regards to finding a humorous biblical incident.

The Bible says: *I will bless her and will surely give you a son by her. I will bless her so that she will be the mother of nations; kings of peoples will come from her."* Abraham fell facedown; he laughed and said to himself, *"Will a son be born to a man a hundred years old? Will Sarah bear a child at the age of ninety?" And Abraham said to God, "If only Ishmael might live under your blessing!"* (Genesis 17:16–18, NIV)

And:

*Then the LORD said, "I will surely return to you about this time next year, and Sarah your wife will have a son." Now Sarah was listening at the entrance to the tent, which was behind him. Abraham and Sarah were already old and well advanced in years, and Sarah was past the age of childbearing. So Sarah laughed to herself as she thought, "After I am worn out and my master is old, will I now have this pleasure?" Then the LORD said to Abraham, "Why did Sarah laugh and say, 'Will I really have a child, now that I am old?' Is anything too hard for the LORD? I will return to you at the appointed time next year and Sarah will have a son." Sarah was afraid, so she lied and said, "I did not laugh." But he said, "Yes, you did laugh."* (Genesis 18:10–15, NIV)

Those less inclined to laugh will say the characters showed a lack of trust or faith in God. There is faith and then there is, in the words of Arnold on *Diff'rent Strokes*, "Whatchu talkin' 'bout, Willis?"

She made a difficult situation light. Not to have a child, for many women, especially during this time in history, was devastating. A woman who was barren was almost considered an outcast. As can be seen with Hannah in the first book of Samuel:

The Bible says: *But to Hannah he would give a double portion, for he loved Hannah, although the LORD had closed her womb. And her rival also provoked her severely, to make her miserable, because the LORD had closed her womb.* (1 Samuel 1:5–6, NIV)

*Then Elkanah her husband said to her, "Hannah, why do you weep? Why do you not eat? And why is your heart grieved? Am I not better to you than ten sons?" So Hannah arose after they had finished eating and drinking in Shiloh. Now Eli the priest was sitting on the seat by the doorpost of the tabernacle of the LORD. And she was in bitterness of soul, and prayed to the LORD and wept in anguish. Then she made a vow and said, "O LORD of hosts, if You will indeed look on the affliction of Your maidservant and remember me, and not forget Your maidservant, but will give Your maidservant a male child . . .* (1 Samuel 1:8–11, NIV)

Similarly to Sarah, Hannah's outcome was also fruitful. However, the point of the previous illustration—that being barren was considered shameful and extremely hurtful for women who could not conceive and bear children—is hopefully not lost.

So instead of Sarah just blurting out, "I can't have children.

I'm barren, you blooming idiot," she could have gone a little further and said, "And in case you didn't notice . . . I'm old!!!"

What many forget is that Sarah was not the first to laugh at this promise of childbearing. Abraham was given the same promise and he fell on his face on the ground laughing. This might have been a little embarrassing for them both as well. After all, this was not an immaculate conception. Even though Sarah may have referred to herself as "worn out," it does not mean Old Abe agreed.

Later on Sarah makes a profound statement that we readily agree with: *"God hath made me to laugh; every one that hears will laugh with me"* (Genesis 21:6).

What we may mistake as laughter of unbelief could have also been laughter of relief. This would be similar to someone who receives unexpected good news that a disease they had or financial distress they thought they were in is nonexistent. They might exclaim, "Really? What about the notice I received?" or "What about what the doctor said?"

Is there proof that God laughed with Sarah and Abraham? Interestingly He didn't chastise Sarah for lying about laughing. Some would think He'd be angry for their unbelief or response. Even more important, God seems to join in the fun by naming their child Isaac, which means "laughter" in Hebrew.

# CHAPTER EIGHT

## Melodies from Heaven?

*Every human being comes from the hand of God,*
*and we all know what is the love of God for us.*

—Mother Teresa

Music. You cannot go into any church experience and not be affected by the music. Music helps to invoke the praises of God's people. David, the most notable praiser in the Bible, time and time again affirmed the value of offering high-sounding praises to God even while in the thick of a "wilderness" experience. Consider that while in the wilderness of Judah, David refused to focus on his dilemma, but rather on his relationship with God (Psalm 63:1–11). Looking at David's results, it would seem that the Christian believer should learn to give a shout of praise to the Lord even when it *seems* hopeless.

Praise flows from our friendship with God. People who praise God on a regular basis do so because they have found the Lord to be altogether lovely and they can't stop thinking of Him and talking about Him. Praise is a conscious choice. Praise is an act of your will. When you offer God true praise, you make a conscious decision to commend, approve and glorify Him. Praise, therefore, is not based on your emotions or feelings. Praise is a willing sacrifice. Praise becomes a sacrifice when you offer your praise to God just because He deserves and asks you to do it. You may not feel like praising Him, and in truth, it may be quite difficult for you to look beyond the difficulties or problems in your life. Yet when you choose to open your lips—in glory to God—and speak forth your adoration, gratitude and thanksgiving to God, not only do you feel better, but you please Him. What did Job do? In all that he had been through—he worshipped God. And praise is an expression of faith. Faith without works is dead (James 2:17). God sees your faith (invisible) but man sees your works (visible). Therefore, praise that is in the heart but not expressed is dead. Faith is the highest act of praise, and praise is the highest form of faith.

The hymns of the church were borne out of the deep, personal and often tragic experiences of their writers. They do, with great conviction, convey the sovereign power of God and His faithfulness to meet every variety of need. When David repented of his adulterous relationship with Bathsheba, he petitioned God to open his mouth so that he might sing a hymn to His honor (Psalm 40:3). Unfortunately, all the music we hear sung in church is not sung by the most melodious of voices, and because of that fact, laughter almost always finds its way in when the, ummm, voices are not so heavenly. I've often wondered if Jesus changes the sound before it gets to the heavenly throne.

Either way, true praise comes from our hearts so I'm sure, to God, it doesn't matter how you sound, or what others may think, for God loves to inhabit the praises of His people.

*The time to relax is when you don't have time for it.*

—Sydney J. Harris

## HE WILL GIVE YOU REST . . .

I had just returned to my home in Detroit from a long week of singing. It had been a week of getting up early to catch a plane, getting to sound checks, late concerts each night. This was night after night for a week and, to say the least, I was TIRED! Mother Boyd was preaching in Detroit that night and I was to sing. The Spirit began to move and Mother Boyd began laying hands and praying for people, or as we call it, "Shootin' people up." I was on the stage when she got to me. . . . She SHOT ME UP and I fell down by the piano and was really out in the Spirit! As I came to myself, I realized I had rolled up under the piano and gone to sleep! As the sisters were getting me up, I saw the Spirit was high up in there. I DID NOT want them to know what happened so I said, "PRAISE HIM!"

**Vanessa Bell Armstrong** is an award-winning gospel singer who released her debut album *Peace Be Still* in 1983. Her most famous songs include "You Bring Out the Best in Me" and "Pressing On."

The Bible says: *"Come to me, all you who are weary and burdened, and I will give you rest. Take my yoke upon you and learn from me, for I am gentle and humble in heart, and you will find rest for your souls. For my yoke is easy and my burden is light."* At that time Jesus went through the grainfields on the Sabbath. His disciples were hungry and began to pick some heads of grain and eat them. (Matthew 11:28–12:1, NIV)

## Reflection

In the previous Bible passage, it's interesting that most have not noticed the continuance of Jesus's thought because of the chapter break. It appears that Jesus is speaking to his disciples and audience about true rest that surpasses what the body gets. It can't be provided by one day or a vacation or a retirement. The truest of rest comes when we are at peace in our spirit with God. In the meantime, get some sleep, just not under a piano.

*Unity without verity or truth is no better than conspiracy.*

—Puritan John Trapp

## THE PIANO SPELL

Most church members have experienced a service when the glory of the Lord so filled the house you felt that you could accomplish anything because of the power of God. Just recently, my church had that experience where the Holy Ghost fell so heavy that it was like the Day of Pentecost.

Well, again, I wasn't born, but my mom told me that many years ago she was at church and it was a Holy Ghost–laden service. It was on a Saturday afternoon and the Holy Spirit was high. The glory of the Lord had filled the house. And the unified body of believers were praising and worshipping God. All of a sudden, out of nowhere, two members of the church, Bro. Williams and Bro. Mack, also felt the Spirit at the same time. They felt the Spirit in such unity that, at the same time, both of them jumped on the piano stool and began to play—terribly. They had no sense of timing, no sense of rhythm, no sense of notes. Nothing. The piano playing was so awful it actually quenched the Spirit.

The congregation was stunned. There were no more joyous shouts, dancing in the aisles nor hand clapping. Everyone just stared at these two brothers who had, for whatever reason, felt the unction, together interestingly, to play the piano. The pastor stepped out of the pulpit and graciously escorted them back to their seats.

**Reverend Patricia S. Webster** is the senior pastor of Shiloh Pentecostal Church, Inc.–Christian Love Center in Somerville, New Jersey, and is also the mother of the author.

The Bible says: *In everything give thanks; for this is the will of God in Christ Jesus for you. Do not quench the Spirit.* (1 Thessalonians 5:18–19)

## Reflection

The choices we make in life, whether right or wrong, are seemingly reinforced when another person or people join forces with these decisions. It's as if the doubt that may have been present beforehand is extinguished simply because someone else has decided that opinion was correct. Of course, the more people join in this way, the more likely we are not to hear any counterpoints.

Must we forget that a large portion of Germany supported the Nazis. That Columbus was accompanied by experienced sailors and still couldn't find India. Collective minds on an idea is not a guarantee of righteousness.

We should always continue to seek guidance and not close our hearts and minds to other ideas, because although one hundred may be of one opinion, there may be one other way that is still God's alone.

*The final test of a leader is that he leaves behind him in other men the conviction and the will to carry on.*

—Walter Lippmann

## SWING LOW, SWEET . . . CHARIOT?

It seemed like just another Sunday service. Don't they all? On this particular Sunday morning a man came in and rode his bike up the center aisle—everyone just stopped and looked, as they were in their devotional at that time. Apparently he was in the wrong church, as he just turned around and rode his bike back out of the worship center.

Pastor Joel Rudolph still to this day does not know how the man got past the ushers. He probably wasn't noticed because in today's church riding a bike into the church is quite normal . . . somewhere. Fortunately he never came back. Perhaps he found the right . . . path.

**Apostle Joel Rudolph** is the senior pastor of Christian Fellowship Center in Paterson, New Jersey.

The Bible says: *As they were walking along and talking together, suddenly a chariot of fire and horses of fire appeared and separated the two of them, and Elijah went up to heaven in a whirlwind. Elisha saw this and cried out, "My father! My father! The chariots and horsemen of Israel!" And Elisha saw him no more.* (2 Kings 2:11–12, NIV)

## Reflection

Expect the unexpected. We are taught and told that we are to expect these little interruptions in our daily lives. Sometimes these interruptions can be minor inconveniences and at other times they can be extremely untimely. While Elijah's departure might have felt like a major untimely event to Elisha, it served a greater purpose. His purpose is not always clear. It's possible many will be understood until the "by and by." Even when a bike rides down the aisle of a church.

# *Laugh Stop*

### Rawhide

An elderly gentleman had fallen asleep during the church service. All of a sudden in the middle of the sermon the man yelled, "Head off that stampede!" The man was dreaming about the movie *Rawhide* and thought he was the principal character, Rowdy Yates.

The Bible says: *Your old men will dream dreams.* (Joel 2:28)

### Catch the Fire

About thirty years ago an altar boy's gown caught on fire during a Christmas service. Apparently when you mix preadolescent boys, flammable gowns and candles, there's great potential for conflagration. The priest was the first to notice the flames. Most in the congregation were not paying attention. Abruptly their attentions were brought back to the altar when the priest knocked the startled altar boy to the floor and began rolling him around to put him out. The other altar boys got involved in variously inept ways, ranging from throwing their own bodies on their smoky cohort to racing for the holy water. Meanwhile, the altar boy's mother fainted. The ushers worked at reviving mom—largely by fanning her with their collection baskets—while her son stripped down to his Skivvies, right there on the altar.

> *His word is in my heart like a fire, a fire shut up in my bones. I am weary of holding it in; indeed, I cannot.* (Jeremiah 20:9)

> *Laughter is the sun that drives winter from the human face.*
>
> —Victor Hugo

## BRINGING IN THE SHEEP

Many can recall a plethora of church songs that they learned as young children and will forever be engraved in their minds and hearts. "Jesus Loves the Little Children," "Amazing Grace," "Silent Night" and "Bringing in the Sheaves" are some of the traditional songs that have been sung during Sunday morning worship. I'm a hymn lover—always have been—but with the new wave of gospel music, some of the more traditional songs have been revised with a more modernistic approach and have attracted a legion of gospel music fans who may not "vibe" with the more traditional version. One Sunday morning while I was enjoying church, one of these traditional songs received a face-lift that no one expected.

My pastor had preached, the altar call had been given and, as is customary at this church, we had a "praise break" before the benediction that was given by one of the praise and worship leaders. Well, this particular Sunday, the praise and worship leader was unavailable, so Pastor Pat asked for a volunteer. Don't you know when you ask for a volunteer, be prepared for anything to happen. One of the church members raised her hand and said, "I'll do it, Pastor!" As she was walking up to the microphone, she started talking about how one of the church members was doing well by bringing in sheep for the Lord, how the pastor was a great example of witnessing, and then all of a sudden she started singing a new hymn, "Bringing in the sheep, bringing in the sheep, we will come rejoicing, bringing in the sheep!" My cousin was sitting in the same row with me and I said to him, "It's bringing in the sheep? I thought it was bringing in the sheaves." Soon ad libs of "sheep, sheep, sheep" were heard within the congregational choir and the ripples of giggles soon turned to rivers of laughter as she sang at the top of her lungs the wrong words—much to the surprise of the congregation.

Since most of us don't know what sheaves are, maybe "Bringing in the Sheep" isn't such a bad idea.

**Patti S. Webster** is the CEO of W&W Public Relations, Inc., and a member of Shiloh Pentecostal Church, Inc.-Christian Love Center in Somerville, New Jersey.

The Bible says: *O sing unto the Lord a new song: sing unto the Lord, all the earth.* (Psalm 96:1)

## Reflection

The Bible tells us that we should "sing unto the Lord a new song." And although funny, the premise behind "bringing in the sheep" is one that we should all live by. As we are followers of Christ, our lives should be a reflection of Jesus Christ, the one we serve and in whom we believe. When we live lives that reflect the glory of God, there will be a new melody in our hearts, and even though it may start out to be what some consider a funny rendition of a favorite hymn, it will turn out to be a new song that will draw us closer to the heart of God.

**Note:** "Bringing in the Sheaves" is an excellent classic hymn written by Knowles Shaw, who was inspired by Psalm 126:6: "He who goes out weeping, carrying seed to sow, will return with songs of joy, carrying sheaves with him."

*I generally avoid temptation unless I can't resist it.*

—Mae West, *My Little Chickadee*

## IT'S GETTING HOT IN HERE!

As time has gone on within the Pentecostal culture, there have been some minor improvements. However, there are those churches that have had difficulty in releasing old traditions. They primarily focus on clothing. Modesty is the key. Typically they will utilize a "lap cloth," which is like a big sheet in some cases, to cover a woman's bare legs in the event of spiritual excitement and the unfavorable showing of too much skin.

There was a time back in the midnineties that I had to play at a tiny church in downtown Orlando. It was hot and typically humid. It was your typical charismatic, holiness church where revival was going on.

Anyhow, it was my time to minister and I'll never forget it. I had on a brown suit—a skirt that was JUST above my knees and a matching jacket. I sat down at the keyboard and began to play and sing. I was sweating in that hot little church! And a woman came over to me and passed me a rather large cloth. So I took it into my hands and wiped my face with it and laid it on the keyboard in front of me. Minutes later, she came over to me, took up my extra large cloth and passed it to me again.

I was puzzled because I didn't know what she was suggesting. After church, we went to eat . . . as you know we all do after a revival! And at the table, my family was laughing at me, telling me that I used my "lap cloth" for a sweat rag at those people's church!

**Ayiesha Woods** is a popular contemporary Christian music artist. In 2004, she won "Producer of the Year" at The Caribbean Gospel Music Awards (better known as the Marlin Awards). Ayiesha has been nominated for a Grammy in the category "Best Pop/Contemporary Gospel Album." Her next album, currently untitled, is slated to release in May 2008.

The Bible says: *Open the gates that the righteous nation may enter, the nation that keeps faith. You will keep in perfect peace him whose mind is steadfast, because he trusts in you. Trust in the LORD forever, for the LORD, the LORD, is the Rock eternal.* (Isaiah 26:2–4, NIV)

## Reflection

It's interesting how our minds can float away from what's good. On many occasions we do the exact opposite of that old axiom "Eat the meat and throw out the bone." We, in fact, will gnaw on the bone. In the previous story, the concentration was on an innocent young girl's fashion sense rather than the beautiful melody she was making to the Lord. Maybe if they had employed air-conditioning, then it might not have been so hot in there.

# *Laugh Stop*

### And Now a Commercial Announcement

A little girl went to church for the first time. As she was leaving with her parents, the minister asked how she had liked church. "I liked the music," she replied, "but the commercial was too long."

### Adam, Eve and the Station Wagon

A teacher asked her students to draw a picture of their favorite Old Testament story, and as she moved around the class, she saw there were many wonderful drawings being done. Then she came across a boy who had drawn an old man driving what looked like a station wagon. In the backseat were two passengers, both apparently naked.

"It's a lovely picture," said the teacher, "but which story does it tell?" The boy replied. "Doesn't it say in the Bible that God drove Adam and Eve out of the Garden of Eden?"

### Have Communion Your Way!

The church was celebrating Communion. During the "children's sermon," the minister was talking about Communion and what it is all about. "The Bible talks of Holy Communion being a 'joyful feast.' What does that mean? Well, 'joyful' means happy, right? And a feast is a meal. So a 'joyful feast' is a happy meal. And what are the three things we need for a happy meal?" A little boy put up his hand and said, "Hamburger, fries and a regular soft drink?"

*The most wasted of all days is one without laughter.*

—e. e. Cummings

## THE CHURCH LIMBO

On Sunday mornings at my church, we have Sunday Bible School, congregational prayer then Sunday Morning Worship. It's a pretty normal routine that the members of the church and visitors go to the altar for congregational prayer immediately following Sunday School before going to their seats for worship service. While the shifting is going on, the ushers on duty prepare the sanctuary so that everyone will be seated quickly. The ushers also secure the middle aisle (customary in most churches) with a simple red velvet rope hung between two chairs.

Never a Sunday goes by when one member of the congregation isn't begging an usher to allow him or her to walk down the middle aisle, since he or she is seated close to that end of the pew. The member doesn't want to take the loooooong walk over twenty pairs of legs to exit the sanctuary. But the ushers are diligent in their work in making sure the aisle stays clear, and those who need to move sit on the other end.

As a deacon, I have an assigned seat that is usually on the last row next to where the rope is placed. This particular Sunday morning, as I was preparing for service, I couldn't believe what I saw. Instead of walking around, as he should have, the church member did the unexpected—he decided to limbo under the rope and then proceeded to his seat. There's nothing like seeing a forty-five-year-old man limbo while holding in your laughter during service.

I will have our church band break out with Calypso music the next time this opportunity presents itself.

**Patti S. Webster** is the CEO of W&W Public Relations, Inc., and a member of Shiloh Pentecostal Church, Inc.–Christian Love Center in Somerville, New Jersey.

The Bible says: *If ye love me, keep my commandments.* (John 14:15)

## Reflection

In life it's so easy to bend the rules when one feels that the rules are easy to bend. It's easy to speed when everybody else is speeding. It's easy to take an extra ten minutes for lunch when everybody does. It's easy to walk down the center aisle at church, even though you are asked not to. The problem is, one act of disobedience, great or small, can lead to another and another and another. And even the smallest act of disobedience is sin to God. The Bible talks about following the rules of both God and man. As we strive to live a Godly life, we must understand that we must be honorable in both word and deed. The smallest act of disobedience can put our feet on the wrong path, but the smallest act of obedience proves our desire to please God in all that we do.

*I still say a church steeple with a lightning rod on top shows a lack of confidence.*

—Doug McLeod

## OH MAGNIFY THE LORD

I was visiting a church, and during the praise and worship, a woman was dancing in the Spirit. She danced her way right next to the pew I was sitting in, although, mind you, I was on the end of the pew. I saw the somewhat large woman beginning to fall backward with no indication of trying to catch herself. So, as most people would do, out of pure reflex, I put my arm out to break her fall. (Remember I said she was, ummmm, large.) By engaging my bicep to break her fall, I practically created a human jack and she lifted my entire body off the pew, through the air and onto her. So here's the scene: this very large woman (nothing against my full-figured sisters), slain in the Spirit, skirt up beyond the level of comfort—now with me on top of her in the perfect position to procreate if the location, mood and circumstances were different. The choir, never missing a beat, continued singing, "Oh Magnify the Lord." I just wish they had left out the part about "letting us exalt His name together," at least for now.

Interestingly, I don't think she ever found out that we had gotten so close.

**Reverend Walter R. Harrison** is a pastor at Emanuel Temple in Florida.

The Bible says: *My soul shall make its boast in the LORD; The humble shall hear of it and be glad. Oh, magnify the LORD with me, And let us exalt His name together.* (Psalm 34:2–4, NIV)

## Reflection

There's an old saying, "We are to dance with the one we came with." Unfortunately we are placed in situations beyond our control and embarrassing situations develop, and we end up encountering something we had no way of preventing. "How do I explain this situation to my church, to my spouse, to my friends?" we may say. This is a natural reaction. However, maybe we should strive to have a spiritual reaction and realize that the God who allows us to get into sticky spots is the same one who will explain it to our loved ones.

# *Laugh Stop*

### The Hushers

Six-year-old Angie and her four-year-old brother, Joel, were sitting together in church. Joel giggled, sang and talked out loud. Finally, his big sister had had enough. "You're not supposed to talk out loud in church," she hissed. "Why? Who's going to stop me?" Joel asked. Angie pointed to the back of the church and said, "See those two men standing by the door? They're hushers."

### God's E-Mail

I had been teaching my three-year-old daughter, Caitlin, the Lord's Prayer for several evenings at bedtime. She would repeat after me the lines from the prayer. Finally, she decided to go solo. I listened with pride as she carefully enunciated each word, right up to the end of the prayer: "Lead us not into temptation," she prayed, "but deliver us from e-mail."

*When the Angels arrive, the devils leave.*

—Egyptian Proverb

## SHAKE THE DEVIL OFF!

It was one of those hot revivals. Our church of normally two hundred people had swelled to approximately four hundred. The balcony was packed, the front choir one and the back one over the entrance. The pulpit was full of the heavyweight ministers who had been brought in for the revival.

It was at this time that the church was rocking. We were singing Dorothy Norwood's classic "Shake the Devil Off." The crowd seemed to be into it more than usual. "He's under my feet/Shake the devil off. He's under my feet/Shake the devil off. In the name of Jesus shake the devil . . ." And right then a bat flew out of the pulpit. All these great men of God who were just singing about shaking the devil off made a beeline for the door.

With all the excitement going on, someone decided the best way to catch the bat would be to cut the lights off. Huh??? Eventually the lights were cut back on and a deacon saw the bat under one of the chairs on the pulpit and went to retrieve it. Ouch!!! The bat bit him. Someone decided to kill it, but was stopped so that they could go and have it checked for rabies. Fortunately no rabies and they are still shaking the devil . . . or the bat off.

**Patti LaBelle** is a popular Grammy Award—winning R&B and gospel singer and songwriter, as well as an actress. She has led two groups, Patti LaBelle & the Bluebelles, and Labelle. She is best known for her passionate stage performances, wide vocal range and distinctive high-octave belting. Her biography, *Don't Block the Blessings,* remained at the top of the *New York Times* best-seller list for several weeks. She is also a best-selling cookbook author.

The Bible says: *The white owl, the desert owl, the osprey, the stork, any kind of heron, the hoopoe and the bat. All flying insects that walk on all fours are to be detestable to you.* (Leviticus 11:18–20, NIV)

## Reflection

Reality is much different from fantasy. While it is true that "greater is He that is in me than he that is in the world," we really don't want to experience the dark side on a personal level. It would probably have most of us running like . . . a bat out of hell.

*Man plans and God laughs.*

—Jewish Proverb

## A SONG IN MY HEART

Music is an integral part of the Christian worship experience. No matter what religion or belief, everyone will agree that there is no better place to hear musical sounds and songs of praise and worship than at church. On this particular Sunday, however, the congregation had no idea that the song they were about to hear would forever change the face of morning worship.

Not long ago at a church in Washington, D.C., they were having praise and worship service. During the praise and worship time, the leader noticed that one of the old church mothers they hadn't seen in some time had come into the sanctuary. As the story goes, the church mother had been "put away" for a while . . . so the congregation was ecstatic that she was finally home. Since it had been such a long time since they'd heard her sing—she was said to have an incredible voice—the praise and worship leader asked the church mother if she would come up and render a song as a celebration of her homecoming.

Happily, the church mother got up and said she was delighted to be called to render a selection as she'd had a song in her spirit ever since she had "gone away." So she stood in front of the microphone, asked the piano player to play her an intro, and she opened her mouth to sing the song she wanted to share for months: "Three blind mice, three blind mice, see how they run, see how they run . . ." There was not a dry eye in the church as laughter overwhelmed the congregation—but the church mother never stopped singing until the song was done.

**Richard Smallwood** is a world-class composer, pianist and arranger who has clearly and solidly changed the face of gospel music. He can impeccably blend classical movements with traditional gospel, and arrive at a mix that is invariably Smallwood's alone. A diverse and innovative artist, he has achieved many honors; Dove Awards, Stellar Awards and a Grammy also attest to his talents.

The Bible says: *Woe to you, blind guides, who say, "Whoever swears by the temple, it is nothing; but whoever swears by the gold of the temple, he is obliged to perform it."* (Matthew 23:16, NIV)

## Reflection

Although "Three Blind Mice" was not a song that you would normally have listed in the Sunday Morning Bulletin, it can give one an interesting analogy of Christian blindness. Maybe our dear church mother here had a deeper intent to the song . . . and again maybe she was just a little "touched" in the head.

# Humor in the Bible

## Balaam and the Donkey

We've all had those private moments of frustration when objects, whether animate or inanimate, living or nonliving, seem to be going against our way. Typically we take our anger out on these unintelligible things.

If you don't think this is funny, then you need a heart transplant. To fully grasp the hilarity of it, a visualizing is most definitely mandatory.

The Bible says: *Balaam got up in the morning, saddled his donkey and went with the princes of Moab. But God was very angry when he went, and the angel of the LORD stood in the road to oppose him. Balaam was riding on his donkey, and his two servants were with him. When the donkey saw the angel of the LORD standing in the road with a drawn sword in his hand, she turned off the road into a field. Balaam beat her to get her back on the road. Then the angel of the LORD stood in a narrow path between two vineyards, with walls on both sides. When the donkey saw the angel of the LORD, she pressed close to the wall, crushing Balaam's foot against it. So he beat her again.*

*Then the angel of the LORD moved on ahead and stood in a narrow place where there was no room to turn, either to the right or to the left. When the donkey saw the angel of the LORD, she lay down under Balaam, and he was angry and beat her with his staff. Then the LORD opened the donkey's mouth, and she said to Balaam, "What have I done to you to make you beat me these three times?" Balaam answered the donkey, "You have made a fool of me! If I had a sword in my hand, I would kill you right now." The donkey said to Balaam, "Am I not your own donkey, which you have always ridden, to this day? Have I been in the habit of doing this to you?" "No," he said.* (Numbers 22:30, NIV)

Balaam started off fighting to get the donkey back onto the road. Then the donkey stepped onto his foot. Ouch!!! Then the donkey lay down while he was on top riding. He was so furious that when the donkey spoke to him, it didn't even freak him out. You'd think he would have said, "What . . . you can talk?" Instead his response is, "You have made a fool of me!" Imagine that and forgive my paraphrase. Balaam says to the donkey, "Stop messing with me! If I only had a sword, I would smack you really good!"

These are some of the moments that have to be seen. We are left to wonder what happened to the servants who were with him. Were they snickering in the background?

Of course, the message is not lost here. Balaam was disobedient and this was God's way of getting him back on track with the use of an angel and a talking donkey. You have to won-

der if and hope that Balaam and his servants had a good laugh
about this later.

So the next time you bump your head under the sink, drop
a screwdriver under the car or have a stubborn donkey, stop
and think for a second. God may be trying to speak to you.


## Just Cut It Off

Paul fully understood the circumcision procedure. Not only
the outcome, in regards to the decapitation of foreskin, but also
the methodology in actually performing the operation. He considered it a gruesome act. Not that he didn't appreciate the Old
Testament, because he did. He also understood that to be close
to God and one of His children in spirit would not require the
carving of one's flesh. His respect for the traditions of his fathers
passed down from Abraham is evident, as he is described as performing the procedure on one of his own followers, Timothy:

> *Paul wanted to take him along on the journey, so he cir-*
> *cumcised him because of the Jews who lived in that area,*
> *for they all knew that his father was a Greek.* (Acts 16:3,
> NIV)

To further understand Paul, one must understand not only
his theology, but his place in history. While not enthusiastically received in his own time, he is given the credit for spreading this offshoot of Judaism to the non-Semitic world to which
he was accustomed.

Paul himself was a Roman citizen. Not only a Roman citizen, but it appears that he had access to the finer things in life, such as finances, education, contacts and strong trade skills. There has been much debate and speculation that although he attributed himself as being Jewish, in fact from the defunct tribe of Benjamin, he did not grow up in its stricter traditions. There were rumors that he himself, early into his adulthood, acquiesced to the operation. This was done, as legend states, to gain the hand in marriage of a priest's daughter. This would possibly explain his later antagonism toward circumcision. Obviously having this surgery done during one's adulthood is not as enticing as having it done when you're eight days old.

Whatever the reason, it was apparent that he was no great fan of this ritual. His enemies definitely would say he went to a new low when he told his opposers, in the following passage, to just castrate themselves altogether. Ouch.

The Bible says: *As for those agitators, I wish they would go the whole way and emasculate themselves!* (Galatians 5:12, NIV)

We're sure Paul really didn't mean this, as he does normally preach a message of love. Even toward one's enemies. His gruesome request only further reflects his disdain for the surgical procedure. In some regards, he equates even the simple procedure, especially on an adult, as castration. You can only wonder if the agitators weren't turned off by his . . . sharpness.

# The Last Laugh

We've got to learn hard things in our lifetime, but it's love that gives you the strength. It's being nice to people and having a lot of fun and **laughing** harder than anything, hopefully every single day of your life.

—Drew Barrymore

A bus carrying only ugly people crashes into an oncoming truck and everyone inside dies. When they get to meet their maker, because of the grief they have experienced, He decides to grant them one wish each before they enter Heaven. They're all lined up, and God asks the first one what her wish is. "I want to be gorgeous." So God snaps His fingers, and it is done. The second one in line hears this and he says, "I want to be gorgeous, too." Another snap of His fingers and the wish is granted. This goes on for a while with each one asking to be gorgeous, but when God is halfway down the line, the last guy in the line starts laughing. When there are only ten people left, this guy is rolling on the floor laughing his head off. Finally, God reaches this last guy and asks him what his wish will be. The guy eventually calms down and says: "Make 'em all ugly again."

So, the next time you are last in line? . . . Smile.

## THE CLOSING SELECTION

There is an old saying, "He who laughs last laughs loudest." By your continued faith in God and your hope for mankind, you will certainly have the last laugh. In between the laughter there will be moments of tears, anger and stress. When the opportunity to laugh presents itself, take advantage. When the Bible tells us to be transformed in our minds and not to be influenced by the outside world, this also includes our churches, which may not understand God's perfect design.

> The Bible says: *Don't be conformed to this world, but be transformed by the renewing of your mind so that you may be able to determine what God's will is—what is proper, pleasing, and perfect.* (Romans 12:2, NIV)

As more religious tradition is dismissed and other religious taboos are forever removed, we move closer to the idea that God had conceived in His creation of mankind so long ago. Tradition tends to block fact. The days of a dull staid church are getting farther and farther away in our rearview mirror. Getting closer is the image of a happy people that the Creator intended for us to be.

Laughter offers a connection, and the church needs this bonding experience as much as the world. When we find humor together, it creates a kinship that is often not possible in other types of emotional displays. As a people of different characteristics and attributes, we can all have that commonality when we watch Charlie Chaplin jump around a boxing ring or avoid a train accident.

Interestingly, psychologists have conducted studies and observed that we tend to laugh longer and harder and in a completely different manner when accompanied by others. The intensity of our fellowships is enhanced when laughter is part of the communion. Laughter is social and contagious.

Oftentimes the greatest gift a loved one can give another is the knowledge that the loved one has been made happy by the other person's contribution. There is hardly a greater dissatisfaction than to know that the gift you've given someone does little to give him or her joy. This must be how God feels when we refuse to see the joy in the life He has given each and every one of us. The joy that this life gives should be ever most abundant in His houses of worship.

Obviously any reader will understand that it is not the intention of this book to take away the seriousness of our houses of prayer and fellowship. Inevitably and unfortunately, they are also hospitals for the soul. A place where a widow can be loved. The financially ruined can have peace. The lonely can find friends. A place where the weary can find solace and rest. Lastly, a place where the hurt can find laughter.